AND He STILL Waits

AND *He* STILL *Waits*

Compiled By:
Trena D. Stephenson

Publisher:
Daughters of Distinction

"And He Still Waits"
Published by Daughters of Distinction

15122 Callohan Ct
Silver Springs, MD 20906 USA

Copyright © 2011 DOFDLLC
Daughters Of Distiniction

All rights reserved. No part of the book may be reproduced in any form without permission in writing from the publisher, except in the case of brief quotations embodied in articles or reviews

Cover Design and Layout: Sarah Thompson
Interior Layout: Ebony Richardson
Editorial: Cynthia D. Thomas

Acknowledgements

With Many Thanks

First, I would like to thank God for being my creator and my all-in-all. To my beautiful daughter who I love dearly, thanks for the love and support you give continually. To my parents, my aunt Pastor Regina Holmes and my extended family, thanks for being there when I needed you the most. To WofGod Inc. staff and affiliates, thanks so much for all you do to hold my arms up. I could not do what I do without you. To my Daughters of Distinction staff you all rock! Thanks for all you do. Now we can breathe a little, but do not get too comfortable though. The ride is just beginning. To my Bishop Myles and First Lady Farrington of Exodus United Ministries, thanks for being such an awesome covering for my ministry team and me. I love you both very much. To the awesome vessel of God who did the forward of this book, Dr. Mary Murray of Fellowship of Love Community Church, your contribution to this project is greatly appreciated. Finally yet importantly, thanks to all my co-authors of this book. I am so Godly proud of you. The best is yet to come for every one of you. God stretched us and made us better vessels of honor for His sake. If I have forgotten anyone, charge my head and not my heart. Thank you, thank you, and thank you.

With Love
Trena

Foreword

To summarize and review the literature presented in this awesome book, the following points bring spiritual impartation and are highlighted:

There is Power in Silence: This section blessed me in that I too agree with Exodus 14:14: "The Lord will fight for you while you keep silent. Not just in some situations but all of those one encounters. If you just keep still and watch God fight for you, there is nothing you could ask for that God would not do. Wisdom is a gift asked for. Without it, that small member in our mouth [the tongue] can cause you to lose all. God has a characteristic of moving when He wants to in order to use circumstances as learning experiences. Moving ahead of God will cause roadblocks on our journey if we do not wait, listen, stand-still, and see the manifestation of God's power in our lives.

Disciple Vs. Fan: is distinctively based upon who we should be in the spectrum of being a follower of Christ. There are many different angles to view as to what a Disciple is but in the summation of definitions, it stands alone to say Disciples are followers of Christ. As born again believers today, we carry that mantle of being a follower, which in turn means we will obey and accept instruction from the instructor, who is Jesus Christ.

The Anointing: enlightens the believer that once we have accepted Jesus Christ as our personal savor the anointing should rest upon our lives. The scripture emphasized in I John 2:20, "And as for you, the anointing which you received from Him abides in you, and you have no need for anyone to teach you, but as His anointing teaches you about all things, and is true and is not a lie, and just as it has taught you, you abided in Him (NASB)," clearly shows that once received, the anointing will teach all truths according to God's Word. Once the Spirit of God comes upon you, you shall receive Power! Once there is an available vessel to be used, God will pour His spirit upon that person to carry out His Will through His word, preaching and teaching as the spirit gives utterance.

Be Free: One of the most important statements made in Be Free, was through the word coming from II Chronicles 3:17, Now the Lord is that Spirit: and where the Spirit of the Lord is, there is liberty. One would have to be connected with the spirit in order to know if He's present. If we state that we want God to reign in our lives, we have to ensure He's ever present in our surroundings and not just in the sanctuary.

Unconditional Love: Shows great parallel between the unmerited favor of love given to us by God and love that is not of God. "Perfect love through God should be shown with all of your soul, mind, and heart. "1 John 4:18 exclaims, "There is no fear in love: but perfect love casteth out fear: because fear hath torment. He that feareth is not made perfect in love." We often associate God as Love, thus as believers we should treat and respect others with unconditional love. Love is what Love does. Love has to be strong enough to go into all of the nations and teach sheep to keep the commandment of God. The author clearly states that, "Loving God will cause you to give him the glory and not try to take it yourself."

Are You Truly Sold Out culminates the book so profoundly. As you wait continuously for what God would have you do in ministry, you must convince yourself to hold on to the profession of our faith. Likewise, be sold out to Jesus in every aspect of ministry regardless of the shadow that comes to block your view to the finish line that we all strive. The example given which brought a broader view of how we should truly be sold out dealt with an item that is sold out in a store. You are so persistent that you will continue to go from store to store and try harder to find what you are looking for. We should treat God that same way. Even if He does not show up when we want Him to, we have to keep Praying until He appears on the scene. This section really blessed me because, if we can see materialistic things as important enough to manage our time to go from one place to another to find what we are in need of, then God's word should outweigh our natural desires.

I have enjoyed presenting a review that would enlighten the readers of this great book. The authors are each determined to bring all into the knowledge of the truth concerning God's Word for today's people.

Dr. Mary Williams-Murray
Co-Pastor
Fellowship of Love Ministries
Church of God in Christ
Hinesville & Savannah Georgia

Table of Contents

Be Open 11

There Is Power In Silence 19

Healing In His Wings 27

Disciple vs. Fan 37

The Anointing - It is He 45

Be Free 55

Bought With A Price 63

Before the Fall (God's Original Design) 71

Awaiting Your Arrival... 81

Unconditional Love 91

Are You Truly Sold Out?....................................... 99

And He Still Waits 105

When One Journey Ends....................................... 113
Another One Begins

Daughters of Distinction

References

Chapter 1

Be Open

Two small words, one simple phrase, yet with huge significance and impact particularly how it relates to God's plan for our lives today. Some time ago, before I came into the knowledge or rather acceptance of Christ as my Lord and Savior, I understood what it meant to be open from a worldly perspective but not from God's perspective. Yet and still, God was patient with me and He allowed me an opportunity to "fumble" my way through until I got absolutely "sick and tired of being sick and tired" and finally relinquished my heart to Him. Even today, I am amazed and simply grateful for God's mercy that caused Him literally to wait on me to choose Him even though He already chose me for His purpose. Being open has a much different meaning for me today than it did back then, and I'll endeavor to share how through these next few paragraphs as I explain just why it is so important to be open to the move of God and the flow of the Holy Spirit.

First, please allow me to backtrack for a moment just to set the tone for what is to come. As a young girl who did not grow up in a church atmosphere, I came into my own through trial and error, developing a keen sense of my own identity apart from Christ. Experiences, atmosphere, education, environment, and upbringing shape many of these attributes, characteristics, and even flaws.

During my journey from youth to adulthood, I learned how to be open to my surroundings and allow myself to wander through this thing we call life with a willingness to receive only, that which was convenient and/or comfortable. Through my journey, I have learned the values of being open and understanding that God's ways are not like ours. His thoughts are not like ours. Both His ways and His thoughts are much higher (**Isaiah 55:8-9**). I want to encourage each reader because now is not the time to close our ears and become dull of hearing or understanding. God is speaking to His children. He is moving by His Spirit and going beyond the tradition of religion, as we know it. He is also doing a "new thing" that even now begins to spring forth as we see and hear the manifestation of things foretold in the word of God such as wars, rumors of wars, and earthquakes in divers places according to **Luke 21:11**. God is telling His children not to be troubled because all of these things must come to pass (**Matthew 24:6**). In the interim, there is still work to do; ministries are still in birthing, the fulfilling of assignments, and blessings to receive from the Lord. We have already seen signs and indicators in our nation's economy, world events, natural disasters and the recent accounts of increased violence and terrorism, but God still sits on the throne. This is where we find hope, in the gospel of Jesus Christ. We must not allow the cares of the world consume us but rather open ourselves to receive God, trust God, and obey God.

<u>Be open to the Power of God's spirit</u>

Now what exactly does that mean? Of course, I understand what that means now, but there was a time when that type of language was foreign to me. Now that God has processed me a bit more, and given me a little understanding, I never want to exclude those who were once where I was in my spiritual walk and relationship with the Lord. Many times, we take things that we do not understand and we content ourselves with being on the other side of knowledge and understanding, or we fear those things that we cannot quite grasp hold. When I first heard about the baptism of the Holy Spirit with the evidence of speaking in other tongues, I was baffled. I could not understand it, the concept was "weird" to me, it did not make natural sense, and once fear took root, it was something that I decided that I did not want any part. Yet, God waited. He knew my fears, my weakness, my doubt, my sin, my flaws, and everything that could possibly come between me developing a relationship with Him. Yet He was still the gentleman and He waited. Realizing and acknowledging that there had to be something greater than what was, some type of "higher power," I began to desire, to thirst after what my soul longed. One day after deciding to follow Jesus, I joined a church home where I could be fed, nurtured, and perfected. One particular day during the altar call, my Pastor spoke of baptism in the Holy Spirit with the evidence of speaking other tongues. Speaking in other tongues? You can just imagine my facial expression for a moment to hear something like this for the first time, but I attempted to open my mind to it. I was very reluctant and still very fearful about "spooky" things that I could not grasp in the natural realm. My Pastor explained that receiving the Holy Spirit was like turning on a light switch. A light is always going to be a light but it does not become effective, it does not do what it was purposed to do until the switch is turned on. It is not operating in its fullness until you flip that switch. If you have a light that is not shining, is not functioning or operating in its purpose. Having the Holy Spirit indwell you is very similar to having a light switch turned on inside of you. The way my Pastor explained the Holy Spirit to me not only made practical sense but also it gave me a visual example that I could totally grasp. I was still slightly reluctant because of fear but I desired to have my light switch turned on.

In the word of God, it states *"And it shall come to pass in the last days, saith God, I will pour out my Spirit upon all flesh: and your sons and your daughters shall prophesy, and your young men shall see visions, and your old men shall dream dreams:" (Acts 2:17 King James Version KJV)*. Now is that time and I urge all of you to be open to what God is saying in these last days as it pertain to the body as well as our individual lives. God is giving instruction, He is creating divine connections to do Kingdom work, and He is providing uncommon resources to those called according to His purpose.

BE OPEN TO THE MOVE OF GOD'S SPIRIT

When you are indwelled by the Spirit of the Lord, God gives spiritual gifts and ordains offices as further explained in the book of

Ephesians. This allows you to tap into the fullness of God and not just be on the outskirts looking in. It is the difference between being a spectator at a sports event versus being an active participant. It is being fully engaged and in tune with God and His voice. It is having a direct fellowship because of a relationship that has been developed through reading His word (which is flesh), communicating with Him (prayer) and through active praise & worship. Being open to the move of God's spirit could be something as simple as getting an unction in your spirit to pick up the phone and contact a distant relative who simply needs an encouraging word in due season. It could also mean going completely against the grain, risking the approval of others in order to follow God. When we do as the bible says and walk according to the spirit and not the flesh, we begin to walk down a path that is narrow (narrow is the gate and wide is the way to destruction) and not always popular. Nevertheless, God says to trust Him, acknowledge Him in all your ways, do not rely on your own understanding, but allow Him to direct your paths (**Proverbs 3:5-6**). When one is sensitive to the move of God, that is when we begin to see and experience the fullness of God in our homes, our marriages, our ministries, our businesses and all that pertains to us in the body of Christ.

Be open to hear God's voice

One day I was going through some serious adversity. I just felt so weak in my spirit, even though I knew the Lord and baptized with the Holy Spirit. I simply felt weak. I could not describe it but it was almost as though I had been in a battle and lost. I was in a place where I just didn't want to be preached to. I could not receive it, and did not want to for that matter. However, I remembered hearing once that every solution to every problem that we will face as a believer is in God's word. I grabbed my bible and popped it open with no specific destination in mind. I landed on a page where there was one small blurb of red in the right hand corner of my bible. Of course, that red stood out because most of us know that this denotes that Jesus was speaking. It read: *"My grace is sufficient for you, for My strength is made perfect in weakness" (II Corinthians 12:9 New King James Version NKJV).* At that moment, I began to feel what was like a rushing wind in my spirit man that built up strength inside of me to endure, go through, stand, and overcome this particular trial. I knew it was the Lord speaking to me through His word and encouraging me with the knowledge that even at my weakest, His strength is made perfect!

Many times, we expect God's voice to be a thunderous loud sound that pierces our very soul and it may very well be. However, don't always look to hear God's voice in a profound manner because you may miss out altogether. Study the book of 1 Kings particularly Chapter 19 that talks about that "still small voice." The word of God says, *"God hath chosen the foolish things of the world to confound the wise; and God hath chosen the weak things of the world to confound the things which are mighty." (I Corinthians 1:27 KJV)*. There have been moments when my young son has spoken a word and I knew it came from the Lord because of confirmation resulting from my reading and meditating on the word of God through the scriptures.

Be open to the "new thing"

"Behold I will do a new thing and it shall spring forth, shall ye not know it." (Isaiah 43:19 KJV).

"Old things have passed away; behold, all things have become new. " (II Corinthians 5:17 KJV).

"Therefore we are buried with him by baptism into death; that like as Christ was raise up from the dead by the glory of the Father, even so we also should walk in newness of life." (Romans 6:4 KJV).

When God is speaking to me directly and I need clarification about a matter, He typically will send confirmation to me in three's. The preceding three scriptures all reference the term "new" and I believe that in these last days God wants us to pay very close attention to the "new thing" that He is springing forth. In a time when our economy is unstable, God is able to make uncommon provisions in a manner that supersedes the world's system. In a time when unemployment is at an all-time high and people are struggling to make ends meet, it is important for the people of God to be open to a "new thing." Just as God made provisions in the past, He will continue to do so. He sent a raven by the brook to feed Elijah. When that dried up He made other provisions for Him by way of a widow who out of obedience to her own instructions given by the Lord, never saw her jar of oil run dry (I Kings 17). In relation to today, God is birthing businesses, opportunities, and ministries in His people and linking them together the same way He did before. As a body of believers, we are to function in unity, helping one another, upholding one another and even providing for one another in time of need. Remember that although we are talking about a "new thing," these are all principals that were established in the earth long before any of us ever got here. God always remains the same. He is our constant in a world of chaos and inconsistency, but His ability to create new opportunities in a time of famine, despair, and drought is nothing short of amazing. I encourage every person reading this to bind the spirit of fear and continue to operate by faith according to God's word. Expect God to show uncommon favor, create new ways out of no way, and enlarge our territory. He is Jehovah Jireh, our provider.

In summary, I pray that God will bestow upon each of you the wisdom and knowledge it is going to take to carry out your assignments in the earthly realm. I pray that you will continue to be open to God and submit to His will for your lives. May God continue to prosper you and keep you in good health even as your soul prospers.

Joy & Blessings!

"Ye rejoice with joy unspeakable and full of glory" (I Peter 1:8 KJV).

About The Author

Joy E. Turner

An author, entrepreneur, musician, speaker, and teacher called by God to minister the gospel through the various gifts given to her by God.

Author: *Joy desires to utilize her writing as a tool for the ministry of healing, deliverance, development, and inspiration. Her first published book "Content... Right Where I Am" (2008) has received several positive reviews and awards. The author has participated in two book tours (Christian Authors on Tour and Women Writers of God's Word) that have allowed her to expand her book ministry while impacting readers to find their true source of contentment in Christ. Additionally, the author has participated in two national anthologies, Victorious Living for Women and Victorious Living for Moms and through them God has enlarged her territory enabling her to impact the body of Christ on a national level. The author also writes as the Baltimore Christian Living Examiner for the local online publication. The writer also manages a blog called RAWC Star Status and has been a guest blogger and writer for numerous publications including Soar Magazine and Breathe Again Magazine.*

Entrepreneur: *Joy is the owner of JETSET Communications & Consulting, a business that launched based on the need that she observed to help other Christian authors self-promote effectively and in excellence. JETSET provides a wide array of marketing and communication services to authors, artists, musicians, businesses and ministries. Some of the services provided through JETSET include press kits, web content, brochure content, bios, articles, ghostwriting and more. The organization also includes a marketing & PR arm that has helped other ministries to gain exposure and to expand their reach in the media (radio, television, print) for the purpose of building God's Kingdom.*

Musician: *Growing up in Baltimore city, Joy was exposed to the fine and creative arts at a very young age after exhibiting a gift for music that was confirmed by her parents and former music instructors. Joy began playing the piano at the age of 3 and continued to develop in that musical gift later adding singing, songwriting, composing, producing, and arranging to her musical arsenal. Little did she know that God was ordaining her not simply to a career in music but a ministry of music that has now been set aside for His glory. Joy is presently the Music Director at Promise Land Church Ministries in Baltimore, MD and is presently working on a CD and book project entitled Unspeakable Joy.*

Speaker and Teacher: *As a participant in the Christian Authors on Tour, the author has been given numerous opportunities to speak and teach on topics such as "Finding Contentment in Singleness", "Dynamics of Praise & Worship" as well as "Writing as a Tool for Ministry" (CAOT Christian Writers Conference – Carnival Cruise 2010). Also in 2010, the author hosted and coordinated the first "Living Victoriously as a Single Mom" workshop in Baltimore, MD especially designed to provide practical and spiritual support to single moms. The author has presented on numerous panel platforms in addition to speaking at other workshops and conferences like the 2010 Worship Conference presented by Set the Captives Free Outreach Center (Pastors Linwood & Karen Bethea.) Additionally the speaker has utilized her vocal gifts as a radio co-host for the Christian Authors on Tour Blog Talk Radio program and a television host for Daughters of Distinction Live (Woman of God Inc. Ministries.)*

Joy believes that God has called her to spread His joy to the entire world by operating in the fullness of the spirit and utilizing all of the gifts & talents that He has given. She shares a burden to minister specifically to those who suffer from depression, low self-esteem and/or have been raped, abused and tormented by a spirit of despair and hopelessness.

"The JOY of the Lord is your strength" – (Nehemiah 8:10 KJV).

Chapter 2

There Is Power In Silence

"If I had not been silenced, I would not have heard you directing my path."

"The Lord will fight for you while you keep silent." (Exodus 14:14 New American Standard NASB).

Lately, I have noticed that there does not seem to be very many people receiving deliverance from various addictions, especially drugs. This is the very demon that I was delivered from years ago. I know that the same demon is still running wild in every city. I was raised in a Christian home of six children; my father was an Elder and a Minister in a holiness church. Like most Christian homes, we had to attend Church every Sunday. I can recall my father always saying, *"Children, if you ever get in trouble, call on the name of Jesus."*

Just before I graduated from secretarial school, I acquired a job at a very affluent law school. I stopped hanging out with my old friends and embraced a new circle of friends: professional people who believed in both working hard and partying hard.

I began to frequent parties where marijuana and alcohol were plentiful. Marijuana became my initial drug of choice; that is, until crack cocaine came on the scene. At first, I was able to maintain a reasonable balance between using drugs and working. However, eventually, my using began to affect my attendance at work and my demeanor around family and friends changed. I noticed that some of the professionals I worked with would disappear for a few weeks, come back, and about two weeks or so later, repeat the cycle all over again.

Eventually, I began taking off from work more and more, for much longer periods. I received letters from my employer asking when I was returning to work, and questioning what was going on with me. During that time, I continued receiving my full pay, which was a very hefty sum. It was not long before I realized that I was hooked! I was addicted to crack cocaine and felt helpless to do anything about it. Every now and then, even in the midst of feeling helpless, my father's words would come back to me, *"If you ever get in trouble, call on the name of Jesus."*

I recall one night that I had gotten tired of the life-style I was living, but I did not know how to stop it. I asked my male friend to go to church with me; he declined and informed me that he only went to church when he visited his parents in North Carolina. By the way, he did not have a clue that I was on drugs, but knew I was in turmoil. About a week later, I asked him again to go to church with me, and again he refused. I immediately went to the bathroom, I looked at myself in the mirror and said, "Lord, that's it, I want him out of here!" Three days later we had an argument (and we never argued about anything) and I asked him to leave.

During the following week, I visited a girlfriend with whom I use to get. I told her that I wanted to change my life-style and that I wanted to go to church. I told her our family was raise in a Christian home and I wanted to change my life style. She confessed that she desired the same thing.

The next day, while sitting in my room, I decided that as soon as I pick up my paycheck that I was going to pay my mortgage note and other bills and I did exactly that. I decided to call my sister, who I call Ms. Silence because she is so quiet. I informed her that I wanted to go to church with her in Baltimore that coming Sunday. Although she worked in Washington, DC, she lived in Baltimore, MD, which meant that I would have to go with her on Friday evening and return home the following Monday.

During the middle of that week, while sitting in my room, I was actually led to contact both of my sisters, Ms. Silence and Ms. Boisterous, which I call my other sister because she is quite out-spoken. I decided that I needed to share with them regarding the situation that I had gotten myself. After contacting them, we agreed on a date and time. However, I felt the need to meet in an open atmosphere. Upon their arrival, they immediately wanted to know what was wrong. I told them that I needed to talk to them privately about a personal matter and that I just wanted the both of them present. We have always met in each other's homes for family issues, gatherings, football games, and various celebrations. When the sisters had important issues to discuss, we would always go to a restaurant. However, this time I was not feeling the restaurant scene or being around a bunch of people. We have never discussed personal or private issues around our children or love ones.

Ms. Boisterous decided that she would do the driving. Our meeting took place on a Wednesday evening, and I really did not have the slightest idea where we were going. As we were driving around and just having girl talk, both sisters suggested various places to have our meeting, but neither one could agree on one place or the other. As we were driving around to find good place to sit and talk, another thought came to mind: "Go to a park-type area." While Ms. Boisterous, continued to drive, I looked up and saw a park. I then said, "What about this park?" and they both agreed to have our meeting there.

We pulled into the park, got out of the car and sat on a bench. I then poured my heart out to them, telling them all that I had been doing. I told them how I had started out smoking marijuana, and thereafter got involved with smoking crack cocaine. The class of people that I was involved with were attorneys and department heads. I told them that I wanted out and needed their help. Once I finished talking Ms. Boisterous said, "Well, I have a friend who runs a rehabilitation center, and I think this would be the ideal place for you to seek help." All I could think about was the people on my job who always went to places such as that, but came back just about the same as they left. I knew that wherever I chose to go, I did not want to keep returning for the same issues, repeatedly. However, my sister,

Ms. Boisterous had pretty much made up her mind about what we were going to do. I got up and walked over to a circle of stones and both sisters followed. As we stood looking at the circle of stones, Ms. Boisterous said, "Well that's it, I will contact my friend next Monday to see when you can get in there." It was then that Ms. Silence spoke and said, "Well, wait a minute; I know a man also, and His name is Jesus." The moment she spoke these words, it hit me in the pit of my belly and I heard myself saying, "That's it, that's it! That's where I want to go."

I went to Baltimore to my sister's Church on an Easter Sunday. The Pastor was preaching a sermon entitled "Resurrection Sunday." Throughout my years of growing up, I had heard many Easter Sunday messages. However, this message was different from any of them. It made me cry; just thinking about the way Jesus was severely beaten, spit upon, and crucified. This message was personal to me. I got in line for prayer, and then went to another area of the church where I was baptized. The next day, I received the Holy Ghost at the Pentecostal Church of Deliverance. From that day forward, I have lived holy before the Lord, and have not turned back! It was the most pivotal time in my life; the time that Jesus had set aside from the moment of my conception.

Upon reflection, what I find most interesting is that my sisters and I have tried to locate that park since the day we went there but, no matter where we looked, we have never been able to locate it again.

What I do realize is that the Lord directs our paths all the way; but as humans, we do not recognize God is silent. However, yet it is He who directs and leads us…in His time.

Silence empowers us to have a clear mind by removing all the mentally stored trash. . We are able to remove the old cobwebs, hatred, and tears of pain. Silence enables us to think more logically and, more importantly, to hear what Jesus has to say to us. We become empowered when we can hear His voice. There is no higher power that can talk to us in that small, still voice that is tuned especially for our ears – none other than Jesus. However, there is an enemy (Satan), who speaks things to clutter our minds – misdirecting us in every possible way.

We cannot hear Jesus until we allow His spiritual vacuum in to clean and remove all that is unlike Him. The more we focus on Jesus, the cleaner, sharper, and more powerful our minds become. We must crucify our flesh and minds daily through the Holy Spirit. We must build upon and preserve these powerful attributes.

His Word is our spiritual cleanser; it enables us to be rooted and grounded in His love. When we are silent, Jesus can speak to us, minister to us and love us so that our faith is strengthened, and we can be made whole. We can then call on Him and He will stand still when He hears our voices, just as He did for Blind Bartimaeus.

Mark 10:45-52 (KJV):

"45For even the Son of man came not to be ministered unto, but to minister, and to give his life a ransom for many. 46And they came to Jericho: and as he went out of Jericho with his disciples and a great number of people, blind Bartimaeus, the son of Timaeus, sat by the highway side begging. 47And when he heard that it was Jesus of Nazareth, he began to cry out, and say, Jesus, thou son of David, have mercy on me. 48And many charged him that he should hold his peace: but he cried the more a great deal, Thou son of David, have mercy on me. 49<u>And Jesus stood still,</u> and commanded him to be called. And they call the blind man, saying unto him, Be of good comfort, rise; he calleth thee. 50And he, casting away his garment, rose, and came to Jesus. 51And Jesus answered and said unto him, What wilt thou that I should do unto thee? The blind man said unto him, Lord, that I might receive my sight. 52And Jesus said unto him, Go thy way; thy faith hath made thee whole. And immediately he received his sight, and followed Jesus in the way."

The point here is that <u>everyone must be still in order to hear.</u> Even Jesus stands still to hear our faintest cries. When Jesus stood still, all became quiet and all were silent. Jesus already knows our needs and desires. Like Blind Bartimaeus, we are called to have faith despite knowing that some people will be healed and some will not; some prayers will be answered and some will not, at least not according to our expectations.

His Word bears this out in **Matthew 7:21-27 (KJV):**
21Not every one that saith unto me, Lord, Lord, shall enter into the king-

dom of heaven; but he that doeth the will of my Father, which is in heaven. ²²Many will say to me in that day, Lord, Lord, have we not prophesied in thy name? and in thy name have cast out devils? and in thy name done many wonderful works? ²³And then will I profess unto them, I never knew you: depart from me, ye that work iniquity. ²⁴Therefore whosoever heareth these sayings of mine, and doeth them, I will liken him unto a wise man, which built his house upon a rock: ²⁵And the rain descended , and the floods came , and the winds blew , and beat upon that house; and it fell not: for it was founded upon a rock. ²⁶And every one that heareth these sayings of mine, and doeth them not, shall be likened unto a foolish man, which built his house upon the sand: ²⁷And the rain descended , and the floods came , and the winds blew , and beat upon that house; and it fell : and great was the fall of it.

    Psalm 26 (KJV) instructs us to "*Be still and know that He is God.*" Jesus gives us instructions all the time, but we cannot hear Him through the "noise of our lives." If we will only be still and know that He is God, He will lighten our load, whatever it may be. "Be still" in the context of this scripture, means to be "quiet" or "silent." Silence is a time of reflection, receiving, and reverence. When He instructs us to be still, it is sometimes the greatest action we can take, and many times the most difficult. Hush, and hear ye Him!

About The Author

Evangelist E. Marie Everhart

Evangelist Marie E. Everhart is a native of Washington, DC. Raised in a Christian home, she is one of six children. She received her formal education in the schools of the District of Columbia, and procured her BA in Computer Science, in 1994 from Strayer University. She later pursued theological studies and graduated from Andersonville Theological Seminary in 2006, where she received her Doctorate of Pastoral Counseling.

For more than 17 years, Evangelist Everhart has diligently and faithfully served at the Pentecostal Church of Deliverance, under the leadership of Pastor Marie E. Brice, in the offices of Usher, Secretary, Sunday School Teacher, and Superintendent. She accepted her call into ministry in the year 2000, and was licensed by Pastor Marie Brice in 2002, where she currently worships and serves in various offices.

Evangelist Everhart is found faithful and true in the house of the Lord. She is compassionate, caring, and sensitive to the needs of the people of God. She has an open door and makes herself available at any time for those who seek counselor who simply need an attentive ear.

Healing In His Wings

But for you who fear my name, the Sun of Righteousness will rise with Healing in His Wings. And you will go free, leaping with joy like calves let out to pasture. (Malachi 4:2 New Living Translation NLT).

Before I begin this journey, let us pray the following prayer.
    Father, I pray that this text will allow the reader to receive healing and direction on the way to the road of recovery. Father, I ask that you expose the enemy for who he is and bring comfort, total healing, and restoration to them. Father I stand in agreement that these evil spirits will not continue to keep your people in silence and bondage because of their past. Father we bind up the silent spirit and release the spirit of authority and forgiveness to rise and live in victory. Father release the breakthrough anointing that will break up every fallow ground that has taken up residence in the hearts of your people, and replace it with yours - a heart full of love, compassion, and forgiveness. Finally, Father give us a new revelation of you as the Son of Righteousness that we may rejoice and go forth leaping over the head of the enemy for he has lost the battle against your people yet again. I thank you that no weapon formed accomplished what it thought it

would. In your Name Jesus, I pray amen.

Healing is the restoration of health; it is a remedy, cure, deliverance, and medicine. It also means to repair and refresh. In order for there to be healing, there has to be some form of brokenness. It could be mentally such as a breakdown in the mind, physically meaning, bodily harm or a breakdown in your health, or emotionally a breakdown in your feelings. Where there is a break in the mind, body, or soul their needs to be healing. The Holy Spirit led me to a prevalent but not popular story in the bible of deceit, rape, abuse, incest, betrayal, and degradation of character to deliver this chapter and passage.

A Story of Betrayal

Second Samuel chapter 13 tells the story of popular King David and his family. King David had two sons named Amnon and Absalom and a daughter named Tamar. Amnon was very obsessed with his beautiful half-sister, Tamar who was a virgin. He was so infatuated with her the bible states that he became sick. "*[1]After this Absalom the son of David had a lovely sister, whose name was Tamar; and Amnon the son of David loved her. [2]Amnon was so distressed over his sister Tamar that he became sick; for she was a virgin. And it was improper for Amnon to do anything to her.*" (II Samuel 13:1-2 NKJV).

Amnon had a very crafty cousin name Jonadab who was also his friend. Jonadab asked his cousin "Why is the King's son moping around all day becoming thinner day after day. What is going on?" Amnon answered, "I am in love with my brother Absalom's sister, Tamar." Now Jonadab the deceitful cousin came up with a scheme and told him what to do. He told Amnon to lie on the bed and pretend to be sick when his father came for a visit. He told Amnon to ask David to allow Tamar to come and take care of him while he was on his sick bed.

Amnon followed Jonadab's advice and pretended to be sick when the King arrived. He asked his father to allow his sister to come over and take care of him. David went home and sent his daughter to take care of her brother. She was to prepare his meals and to feed him. Tamar obeyed King David and went to Amnon's house to take care of him. After cooking for her brother, she took the food to him, but Amnon refused the food. He told her to send everyone else in the household away. After sending everyone away, Amnon told Tamar to bring the food into his bedroom so he can eat from her hand. Tamar obeyed this request and entered Amnon's bedroom to feed him. Upon entering the bedroom, Amnon grabbed his sister's hand and asked her to sleep with him.

She replied, "NO! My brother, do not force me, please do not do this to me, for no such thing should be done in Israel. Do not do this disgraceful thing! Where could I the King's daughter take my shame or show my face after being raped? Amnon people would look at you as a disgrace for doing this sort of thing." Tamar begged him to speak to their dad so he could give her to him in marriage. This was custom in their day. She was desperate to find a solution that would cover them both. However, Amnon was not going to be denied. He ignored her voice.

The result was Amnon raped his sister. Immediately after he raped her he went from loving her to hating her extremely, more than he loved her. Amnon went from being lovesick to pure hatred. WOW! My God, take a breath; breathe and say a prayer. Not only did he violate her, he did not listen to a word she was saying, no reasoning at all. He was all for himself. This was not love. It was LUST. When he got through with her, he told her to get up and get out! Arise and be gone! He did not want to see her face anymore. *"Then he called his servant who attended him, and said, "Here! Put this woman out, away from me, and bolt the door behind her."* (II Samuel 13:17 NKJV). Tamar cried, "NO! Amnon if you throw me out now this will be worse than you raping me, please do not do this to me!" Again, he would not listen. Although violated, she wanted protection from being seen in this state. Unfortunately, Amnon dismissed Tamar and she was abandoned! The way Amnon had his servant throw Tamar out made it look like her appear at fault. She faced degradation, embarrassment, and shame. Tamar put ashes on her head and ripped up her royal clothes before Amnon threw her out because she was defiled. Even though she was very beautiful, she felt dirty, ugly, and did not want to be recognized. She left Amnon's house broken, violated, humiliated, and sobbing bitterly.

By now, you would think this was enough; however, here comes the family betrayal and cover up. Tamar went home where she lived with her other brother Absalom, who loved her also. Upon her arrival, Absalom knew something was wrong. He questioned her, "What happened to you? Has Amnon your brother, been with you? Now listen to this crazy foolishness. He told her for now Tamar hold your peace, keep quiet; do not tell anybody, after all he is your brother. Do not take this thing to heart. There was no regard or respect for Tamar's feelings at all. If this is not the ultimate, then what is? She was told to SHUT UP! What humiliation and betrayal all in the name of family secrets. Absalom wanted to protect the family image while he devised his own scheme. Can you imagine how she felt? Tamar kept quiet and continued to live in her brother's house hidden, bitter, desolate, lonely, and isolated! She was silenced to secrecy. Subsequently, she resided in the darkness and with no identity. We hear nothing further about Tamar (David's daughter) in the bible.

At some point David heard about the entire incident and became enraged. You would think by now daddy was getting ready to handle the issue. Let me tell you that, Daddy does nothing. Daddy loved Amnon his firstborn son so much, even he kept quiet. Although Absalom told Tamar to keep silent, he hated his brother for what he did to his sister. Absalom later killed Amnon and committed treason against his father.

Breaking the code of Silence

Rape is the crime of having forcible sexual intercourse with a non-consenting person. Abuse means to use wrongly, mistreat by inflicting physical or sexual harm, also insulting language. Tamar, Amnon, Absalom, and Jonadab are spirits that are prevalent, alive and functioning today in the form of ABUSE, which I call the best kept secret. It is not just a female thing or a new thing. Abuse has been ongoing for a very longtime. In Amnon, we see three major spirits functioning, the lust of the eye, and lust of the flesh and the pride of life. Being the King's son, he thought he could do what he wanted. Tamar was so beautiful; he wanted his sister at any cost and took what he wanted. Further studies will show these spirits have been in operation since the beginning of time. I am exposing them to get to the root of the matter and give you a better understanding of the thing that is trying to destroy you. Lust is a desire for the forbidden or an obsessive sexual craving. Eve in the garden listening to the serpent's sweet talk challenged what God said about the tree of knowledge in the garden. God said not to eat from that tree. "*When the woman saw that the fruit of the tree was good for food and pleasing to the eye and also desirable for gaining wisdom, she took some and ate it. She also gave some to her husband, and he ate it.*" (Genesis 3:6 New International Version NIV). Satan took advantage of Eve. This marks the beginning of the fall of man. Jonadab represents the crafty spirit, like the serpent suggesting or helping someone do evil. Absalom the silent brother turned avenger and murderer on both the brother and his father.

Rape also means to plunder or destroy. "*The thief does not come except to steal, and to kill, and to destroy. I have come that they may have life, and that they may have it more abundantly.*" (John 10:10 NKJV). In the story, Satan used Amnon as the thief; he stole Tamar's voice, killed her identity, and destroyed her mind.

You or someone you know is in the story of Tamar. One may say, "Well, I have never been raped before," yet at some point in your life, someone took advantage of you. Something traumatic happened to you allowing you to relate to Tamar's emotions. It could have been a relationship gone wrong, a parent giving you away, or a loved one taken from you.

Someone or possibly a situation brought physical or mental harm to you. They hurt you, betrayed you, rejected you, left you for dead, abandoned you, picked on you, or mistreated you. Today, these incidents still affect you. You want love but cannot really give it because of trust issues. You may even be someone who does not know how to say no, because the rapist never heard you saying no. You may go through life needing someone to hear you. You may have love-hate relationships. One minute you love the person and the next minute you want to kill them, be it verbally or physically. Your rape may stand in the way you treat people. You may have even gone from being the victim to becoming the victimizer. You may be blaming yourself and may not like yourself. You may have a major issue with forgiving. You keep ending up in abusive relationships. Maybe you are bitter and lonely. You may be a person of low self-esteem, a person that does not love them self or a person that lives in fear. There are many downfalls to these functioning spirits.

"*Many are the afflictions of the righteous, but the Lord delivers him out of them all.*" (Psalm 34:19 NKJV). Afflict means to torment, hurt, trouble and to distress greatly. It is a condition of physical and emotional abuse. You need to know that Satan's plan is working if you continue to let him win. He does not deserve that power. I pray you gain Godly hatred towards the enemy and declare war on him. Do not go out like Tamar, isolated and in silence. Come out of the reserves and live. Often I find when people are hurt or wounded they go into hiding. It is time to stop hiding and be open. Someone else has experienced the same things as you and you can help prevent others from suffering abuse. Abuse is an epidemic. You need to act now. Acknowledge, confess, and testify to triumph over the adversary.

There is purpose in your pain! There's healing for your mind, body, and soul. You can be free. You are an overcomer and more than a conqueror. God made us to prevail over our inner mess/enemies. I want to make an appeal; there is a relationship worth having with Jesus the King of Kings and the Lord of Lords! He is a Father who is compassionate and sympathizes with us. When your heart is broken and your spirit crushed, the Father is moved.. Believe me, He understands. Jesus can relate because He experienced some of these same experiences too. He was rejected, denied, lied on, spat on, beaten beyond recognition, yet He prevailed for us. Just as there is no valid explanation for some of the things that have happened to you, there was no human reason for Jesus to be, beaten, betrayed and violated either. Imagine how He felt. The same people that called Him Lord are the same people that helped crucify Him. Where Tamar's daddy failed to respond, we have a Father in whom when we cry, He responds. There is something about our cry. Our cry captures Our Father's attention sending Him in pursuit of His children - just as any parent would when hearing their child in distress. "*The Lord is near to those who have a broken heart, And saves such as have a contrite (meaning crushed) spirit.*" (Psalm 34:18 NKJV).

You need to open your mouth and send God a distress signal that the enemy can hear. There is power in His name. When you begin to call on His name, you bring reverence, respect, glory, and honor to Him. He wants to wait on you. Bring it all to Him. The righteous cry and the Lord will hear them. He responds to your cries and your brokenness. The Son has a plan for you. You are on his mind. He wants you free, healed and delivered.

Do not live your life bound by family cover-ups. More importantly, do not cover up what was done to you. God's love is medicine and a powerful healer. There is healing in His wings and they are waiting to scoop you into His presence and cover you with His love. Jesus wants you to know that He is like The Sun a creative energy and life force designed to power you up. He is the Sun of righteousness who rises and sets daily. He rises to light up the world. For every dark night you have, He is the Sun, which is a star that sustains life on earth. You are still here because he has been sustaining you. He is the source of light and heat that sends out glorious radiant beams of light in all directions and from these beams healing flows. He knows where you are, what you have been through, and where He wants to take you.

Psalm 84:11 tells us that, He is a sun and a shield. His wings are the shields, which represent elevation and protection. He has been waiting on us daily, watching over us. There is not a day that He does not rise over you. He rising every day is a guarantee. Rise and be defeated no more. Therefore, the next time you are having a bad day and you want to pull the covers over your head, to block the sun out, remember its Jesus the Son of Righteousness.

I am Angela. I am a survivor of rape, molestation, physical and emotional abuse. I am an advocate for domestic violence and rape victims. The ignoring of the "NO" still bothers me today at times. There are times when I want to say "no" and cannot. Fear grips me at times, and I cannot speak. I become fear's prisoner. There are also times when I am mistreated or wounded, and I cannot talk about it. I go into hiding and remain silent. When these times come, I cry out to my Heavenly Father and His Wings come and scoop me up into His secret place. I stay there while He waits on me. He reminds me that He did not give me a spirit of fear, but of power, love and a sound mind. When this kicks in, I am refreshed and restored. I then mount up with wings of an eagle to fly high above my troubles. I am no longer ashamed of what has happened to me and I certainly will not shut up day or night! He is making me free. I welcome this process. Please understand that whatever happened to you did not just occur. You may have lived with this a long time. It will take one day at a time to bring total healing.

The Sun of Righteousness rises daily to bring you back into right standing with Him. God has placed handpicked professional people to walk me through my journey of healing. Will you not join in the healing? Healing is also God's complete repair of a sinner's soul. God is also a forgiver. Wherever you are in this chapter remember, And He Still Waits with Healing in His Wings!

About The Author

Prophetess Angela Thomas

Angela D. Thomas is employed by Jesus Christ, and is the facilitator of By His Spirit Healing & Deliverance Works. Her mission is to stay a yielded vessel to carry out whatever God desires she do to advance the Kingdom. Prophetess Thomas is fueled with Godly love, driven by people coming to know Him and being made free stating, "I know what it is like to be bound and delivered." Prophetess Thomas is an ordained prophet of Bible way Churches World Wide and A Kingdom Harvest Ministries, under the Leadership of Pastor Floyd Nelson II in Landover, Maryland.

"Once you get free, You will go out leaping with unspeakable joy!"

Chapter 4

Disciple vs. Fan

As this chapter begins, it is important to understand yourself, who and what you are serving. In the times, we live in it is easy to follow the wrong person thing or object when the only one we are to serve or pattern ourselves after is Jesus Christ, our Savior. Once we have evaluated ourselves then we are able to determine what we do and why we do those things. This brings into account our motives and the actions that we take in a day-to-day walk. I realize that all that read this are not on the same level or page in their lives. Therefore, I pray that we all can gain understanding from the word of God regarding this subject, disciple versus fan.

Dictionary.com defines disciple as 1) one of the 12 followers of Jesus Christ; 2) one of the 70 followers sent forth by Jesus Christ Luke 10:1 and as any other professed followers of Jesus Christ in their lifetime. According to the bible dictionary, definition disciple is a scholar, sometimes applied to the followers of: John the Baptist (**Matthew 9:14**), and of the Pharisees (**Matthew 22:16**) but principally to the followers. A disciple of Christ is one who (1) believes his doctrine, (2) rests on his sacrifice, (3) absorbs his spirit, and (4) imitates his example (**Matthew 10:24; Luke 14:26, 27. 33; John 6:69**).

We can gather from these definitions that a disciple is one that is a follower of Jesus Christ. This means that he or she obeys and follows Jesus Christ. This also means that they would have to be a born again believer or as we are often times called a "Christian." Christian means Christ-like in these terms. Being Christ-like is a day-to-day obligation, which is progressive each day. When you are a disciple, you are following someone that you feel can lead you into a place where you cannot lead yourself. There are many examples in the Bible where Jesus Christ had individuals that He calls disciples. The name or title disciple was given because of what they did with Jesus Christ. Let us examine some of the Scriptures to give you clarity. The word "disciple" refers to a learner or follower. The word "apostle" means "one who is sent out." While Jesus was on earth, His twelve followers called disciples. The twelve disciples followed Jesus Christ, learned from Him, and trained by Him. After His resurrection and ascension, Jesus sent the disciples out to be His witnesses (**Matthew 28:18-20; Acts 1:8**) after which they were then referred to as the twelve apostles. However, even when Jesus was still on earth, the terms "disciples" and "apostles" were somewhat used interchangeably.

The original twelve disciples/apostles are listed in Matthew, "*These are the names of the twelve apostles: first, Simon (who is called Peter) and his brother Andrew; James son of Zebedee, and his brother John; Philip and Bartholomew; Thomas and Matthew the tax collector; James son of Alphaeus, and Thaddaeus; Simon the Zealot and Judas Iscariot, who betrayed Him.*" (Matthew 10:2-4 NIV). The Bible also lists the twelve disciples/apostles in **Mark 3:16-19** and **Luke 6:13-16**. A comparison of the three passages reveals a couple of minor differences in the names. It seems that Thaddaeus was also known as "Judas, son of James" (**Luke 6:16**) and Lebbaeus (**Matthew 10:3**). Simon the Zealot was also known as Simon the Canaanite (**Mark 3:18**). Judas Iscariot, who betrayed Jesus, was replaced in the twelve apostles by Matthias (see **Acts 1:20-26**). Some Bible teachers view Matthias as an "invalid" apostle and believe that Paul was God's choice to replace Judas Iscariot as the twelfth apostle.

The twelve disciples/apostles were ordinary men whom God used in an extraordinary manner. Among the twelve were fishermen, a tax collector, and a revolutionary. The Gospels record the constant failings, struggles, and doubts of these twelve men who followed Jesus Christ. After witnessing Jesus' resurrection and ascension into heaven, the Holy Spirit transformed the disciples/apostles into powerful men of God who turned the world upside down (**Acts 17:6**). What was the change? The twelve apostles/disciples had "been with Jesus" – "*Now when they saw the boldness of Peter and John, and perceived that they were unlearned and ignorant men, they marvelled; and they took knowledge of them, that they had been with Jesus.*" (Acts 4:13 KJV). Can the same be said about the modern day followers of Jesus Christ?

After reading these Scriptures, you should be able to see what identifies you as a disciple biblically. Ask yourself these questions of discipleship. Do you consider yourself one that follows Jesus Christ? Have you confessed with your mouth and believed in your heart that Jesus Christ rose from the dead? Have you repented of the sins that would cause you to be a stranger to Jesus Christ?

I have dealt with the subject of discipleship and those who were the early disciples. Now, let us examine the definition of a fan. Dictionary.com, defines a fan as an enthusiastic devotee, follower, or admirer of a sport, pastime, celebrity, etc. However, in this context, we are going to address fan as it can relate to the religious sect. As the definition states, a fan is one who is devoted and can be called a follower. This could so easily be confused with the definition of "disciple" as defined in these terms. You may ask then, "How do they differ" good question. Let me now illustrate in sports how this term is often used. For example, fans may show their enthusiasm or devotion by being a member of a fan club, holding fan events/conventions, or by promoting the object of their interest and attention.

Jesus fed about 15,000 people. He used five loaves of bread and two small fish. He ended up with leftovers to feed the multitude. This was amazing to the people present. They were no longer hungry. They decided that He must be the One because of this loving deed. The people therefore decided to make Him king. These are example of "fans." God recognized that this excitement and eagerness was not one of genuine loyalty. Jesus knew how to respond to His fans. He sent His disciples to the boat, to the lake, to the other side and He headed for the hills. He headed for some solitude. When it was dark and the crowd was asleep and His disciples were in the middle of the lake, He walked out to them. They got to the other side, near home. In the morning, the crowd realized that Jesus was not there. They knew that they were not getting breakfast. They went home, too and they discovered Jesus.

"When did you get here?" the crowd asked as they approached Jesus. *"*^{25}*And when they had found him on the other side of the sea, they said unto him, Rabbi, when camest thou hither? *^{26}*Jesus answered them and said, Verily, verily, I say unto you, Ye seek me, not because ye saw the miracles, but because ye did eat of the loaves, and were filled. *^{27}*Labour not for the meat which perisheth, but for that meat which endureth unto everlasting life, which the Son of man shall give unto you: for him hath God the Father sealed. *^{28}*Then said they unto him, What shall we do, that we might work the works of God? *^{29}*Jesus answered and said unto them, This is the work of God, that ye believe on him whom he hath sent."* (John 6:25-29 KJV).

John says, *^{66}*"From that time many of his disciples went back, and walked no more with him. *^{67}*Then said Jesus unto the twelve, Will ye also go away? *^{68}*Then Simon Peter answered him, Lord, to whom shall we go? Thou hast the words of eternal life. *^{69}*And we believe and are sure that thou art that Christ, the Son of the living God."* (John 6:66-69 KJV).

As these scriptures depict, Jesus had fans, as well as, disciples. Both were in existence in that day as they are today. Fans are the individuals that are in it because of the "thrills." However, to be a true disciple you must be someone that is not just following Jesus Christ to receive. You must be willing to deny yourself in order to be a willing follower of Jesus Christ. You must not be in it because of how you feel it can benefit you. Discipleship is the diligent, deliberate teachings and practices that promote the lifestyle of becoming more like Jesus Christ and imitating the Christ-life in others on a daily basis.

In today's society, with changing trends and popularity stunts, we can see how what seems acceptable can blind individuals. However, we must approach our daily lives in a way that reflects a true dedication to the God that we serve, which is Jesus Christ. We must not allow distortion of the true definition of discipleship by what a fan represents. We often hear people say, "walk the walk, and talk the talk," but who will take a stand for righteousness? The Bible says, *"Follow peace with all men, and holiness, without which no man shall see the Lord."* (Hebrews 12:14 KJV). This scripture must be one that we take into account because when we allow the things that the world does to change how we do things for God and how we view Him; we have become conformed. Refer to Romans *"And be not conformed to this world: but be ye transformed by the renewing of your mind, that ye may prove what is that good, and acceptable, and perfect, will of God."* (Romans 12:2 KJV). As this scripture states, we cannot allow our mindset to be altered by how things appear in this world. A daily transformation must occur in the life of a believer and follower of Jesus Christ. If you noticed, I said a believer and follower, not just one or the other. Let's look at James chapter 1,

"²³For if any be a hearer of the word, and not a doer, he is like unto a man beholding his natural face in a glass: ²⁴For he beholdeth himself, and goeth his way, and straightway forgetteth what manner of man he was." (James 1:23-24 KJV).

What a powerful word stated in this passage, it allows us to pinpoint what our original motives are as it relates to our relationship with God. We cannot just hear the word and not do what it instructs us to do. As a disciple, the Lord expects us to trust what He has instructed us to do through the word of God. However, a fan may say, "Well, I am just going with the flow." However "going with the flow" could simply mean conforming to whatever comes into play within a given situation; which could be good or evil. One must know that when they follow Jesus Christ, he leads in the path of righteousness. *"¹⁴That we henceforth be no more children, tossed to and fro, and carried about with every wind of doctrine, by the sleight of men, and cunning craftiness, whereby they lie in wait to deceive; ¹⁵But speaking the truth in love, may grow up into him in all things, which is the head, even Christ: ¹⁶From whom the whole body fitly joined together and compacted by that which every joint supplieth, according to the effectual working in the measure of every part, maketh increase of the body unto the edifying of itself in love. [17]This I say therefore, and testify in the Lord, that ye henceforth walk not as other Gentiles walk, in the vanity of their mind, [18]Having the understanding darkened, being alienated from the life of God through the ignorance that is in them, because of the blindness of their heart: [19]Who being past feeling have given themselves over unto lasciviousness, to work all uncleanness with greediness. [20]But ye have not so learned Christ; [21]If so be that ye have heard him, and have been taught by him, as the truth is in Jesus: [22]That ye put off concerning the former conversation the old man, which is corrupt according to the deceitful lusts; [23]And be renewed in the spirit of your mind; [24]And that ye put on the new man, which after God is created in righteousness and true holiness."* (Ephesians 4:14-24 KJV).

My prayer is that if you did not know the difference between a disciple and fan; that this reading has enlightened you. As a result, you will make a conscious decision to be a disciple of Jesus Christ and not just a fan because there is a need for true disciples are to spread the life changing Gospel of Jesus Christ, our Lord. May peace and grace be upon you in Jesus' name. Amen.

About The Author

Prophetess Mia Grice-McGee

This multi-faceted woman of God serves in many capacities in the Kingdom, she is a successful entrepreneur, ordained/licensed minister, wife, mother, and the list goes on.. She utilizes the gifts that God has given her through business, education, and ministry.

Mia Grice-McGee was called and chosen at a young age to do God's work. She is the daughter of Charlie Grice, sister of Elvis Grice and Jacqueline McClinton. She holds the honor of being a wife to Corrie; mother of Corrie (Jr.), and Angel; along with being a spiritual mother to many. She cherishes to memory mother, Ethel M. Grice and her first-born son, Devan.

God not only gave her a "vision" for W.A.V.E. Ministries where she is the CEO/President. She also serves or has served in various leadership capacities, including: Founding Pastor/ Overseer of Vision Church of SW Alabama, an Ordained Overseer under the tutelage of Presiding Bishop Wayne (Sr.) and Evangelist Patricia Lacy and works diligently within the Body of Christ.

Mia has spoken on many platforms, and featured on many local and national radio & television stations, including Trinity Broadcasting Network, Cumulus, Clear Channel and Selah TV. She holds various degrees/credentials, including Human Resources Manager/ Independent Business Consultant and Adjunct Professor for various colleges/ universities within the United States and abroad.

Mia often states, "What education I hold is not relevant to the anointing that I possess from God... However, I did receive a Ph.D. (Prophetic, Healing, and Deliverance) from the Holy Ghost, which exceeds my earthly letter(s).

To contact this woman of God, you can go to www.miamcgee.org or

www.waveministries.com;
Mailing address: P.O. Box 82016 Mobile, AL 36689.

Chapter 5

The Anointing It Is He

Your purpose, your calling, your assignments, your giftings are all within destiny. In your destiny is the anointing. One can go through life not knowing whom they are and what they are called to do. Nevertheless, you are an anointed vessel of God, called to fulfill His purposes and plans on the earth.

What is the Anointing?

Simply put, the anointing is the manifested presence of God. The anointing is God Himself manifested. We can see and feel Him. The anointing is the tangible evidence of God. However, feelings do not determine the anointing. You must trust God for the results whether you feel the anointing, or not.

The Purpose of the Anointing

One would have you think the anointing is for a certain few or there is some sort of mystery behind "the anointing," but there is not. I repeat; there is not. The anointing is not a mystery. All born again believers in relationship with Jesus Christ have the anointing. Jesus (Himself) the anointed one resides in you, and God (Himself) lives in us. The problem lies in knowing this and acting on it. What we allow God to do with the anointing is totally up to us as believers. The anointing lives, remains, and dwells in you. The anointing is upon you.

> *"And as for you, <u>the anointing which you received from Him abides in you</u>, and you have no need for anyone to teach you, but as His anointing teaches you about all things, and is true and is not a lie, and just as it has taught you, you abide in Him"* (I John 2:27 NASB). *"[21]Now it is God who makes both us and you stand firm in Christ. <u>He anointed us</u>, [22] set his seal of ownership on us, and put his Spirit in our hearts as a deposit, guaranteeing what is to come."* (II Corinthians 1:21-21 NIV).

Every believer has an anointing that he or she may receive and walk in by faith. The purpose of the anointing is not for us, but for others. We are to bring about change in the lives of people. *"The Spirit of the LORD is <u>upon me</u>, for he has anointed me to bring Good News to the poor. He has sent me to <u>proclaim that captives will be released,</u> <u>that the blind will see,</u> that the <u>oppressed will be set free</u>."* (Luke 4:18 NLT).

God is looking for a willing vessel to flow through. We as believers do not control the anointing; we flow and cooperate with the anointing on the inside of us. We open ourselves to God to so he can use us. When He is ready, He will move. *"[Besides this evidence] it was also established and plainly endorsed by God, Who showed His approval of it by signs and wonders and various miraculous manifestations of [His] power and by imparting the gifts of the Holy Spirit [to the believers] according to His own will."* (Hebrews 2:4 Amplified Bible AMP).

Our part is to hear His voice and be obedient to what He asks of us. He uses our hands, feet, arms, legs, voice, and ears. Do not let God lie dormant on the inside of you. Let God out! Let Him Flow. Let Him heal, deliver, and set free through you!

For Deliverance

> *"It shall come to pass in that day That his burden will be taken away from your shoulder, And his yoke from your neck, And the yoke will be destroyed because of the anointing oil"* (Isaiah. 10:27 NKJ)

For Healing
[12]*"They went out and preached that people should repent. [13]They drove out many demons and anointed many sick people with oil and healed them."* (Mark 6:12-13 NIV).

For Assignments and Gifting
"God never changes his mind when he gives gifts or when he calls someone." (Romans 11:29 Gods Word)

We use our talents and gifts to fulfill God's will in the earth. I believe gifts and talents make the world go around. Our gifts and talents enhance the kingdom. They also cause the kingdom to expand if used in the way God intends, for His purpose.

Every one of us has a destiny to fulfill. God has given you an anointing to fulfill His divine assignment for your personal destiny. When He calls you, He has something for you to do. Your anointing is with purpose and it is inside of you.

There is a catch to the anointing (God's manifested presence) flowing from you and that is: stay with what God has anointed you to do. Only do the task and assignments that God has called you to do. Do not try to be someone else or take on some else's vision.

A dear friend of mine started a church along with her husband. Somewhere in my thinking, I thought the vision was for me too. I wanted to do everything my friend was doing. I felt everything God was giving to them He was giving to me. Assuming since she and I were good friends, automatically I had a say in the ministry, NOT. For the life of me, I could not figure out why I was competing, I could not understand, feelings envious. Not to mention wanting to leave the church and every other week. Things were just not going my way. Out of frustration of trying to sort through my feelings, one day (I will never forget it) God very gently said to me, "I didn't give you the vision, I gave it to them." From that day on, I was free! I stay in my own lane and handle my own assignments. I am doing what God called me to do.

[4-6]*"In this way we are like the various parts of a human body. Each part gets its meaning from the body as a whole, not the other way around. The body we're talking about is Christ's body of chosen people. Each of us finds our meaning and*

function as a part of his body. But as a chopped-off finger or cut-off toe we wouldn't amount to much, would we? So since we find ourselves fashioned into all these excellently formed and marvelously functioning parts in Christ's body, <u>let's just go ahead and be what we were made to be, without enviously or pridefully comparing ourselves with each other, or trying to be something we aren't</u>. ⁶⁻⁸If you preach, just preach God's Message, nothing else; if you help, just help, don't take over; if you teach, stick to your teaching; if you give encouraging guidance, be careful that you don't get bossy; if you're put in charge, don't manipulate; if you're called to give aid to people in distress, keep your eyes open and be quick to respond; if you work with the disadvantaged, don't let yourself get irritated with them or depressed by them. Keep a smile on your face. ⁹⁻¹⁰<u>Love from the center of who you are; don't fake it</u>. Run for dear life from evil; hold on for dear life to good. Be good friends who love deeply; practice playing second fiddle. (Romans 12:4-10 The Message MSG).

<u>God calls and sends Moses to deliver the people out of bondage</u>

Everyone has something to can give back to the community in which they live. Look at how God called Moses.

⁷⁻⁸"God said, "I've taken a good, long look at the affliction of my people in Egypt. I've heard their cries for deliverance from their slave masters; I know all about their pain. And now I have come down to help them, pry them loose from the grip of Egypt, get them out of that country and bring them to a good land with wide-open spaces, a land lush with milk and honey, the land of the Canaanite, the Hittite, the Amorite, the Perizzite, the Hivite, and the Jebusite. ⁹⁻¹⁰"The Israelite cry for help has come to me, and I've seen for myself how cruelly they're being treated by the Egyptians. It's time for you to go back: <u>I'm sending you to Pharaoh to bring my people, the People of Israel, out of Egypt</u>." (Exodus 3:7-10 MSG)

¹⁰Moses raised another objection to GOD: "Master, please, I don't talk well. I've never been good with words, neither before nor af-

ter you spoke to me. I stutter and stammer." ¹¹⁻¹²God said, "And who do you think made the human mouth? And who makes some mute, some deaf, some sighted, some blind? Isn't it I, GOD? So, get going. I'll be right there with you—with your mouth! I'll be right there to teach you what to say." ¹³He said, "Oh, Master, please! Send somebody else!" ¹⁴⁻¹⁷<u>GOD got angry with Moses</u>: "Don't you have a brother, Aaron the Levite? He's good with words, I know he is. He speaks very well. In fact, at this very moment he's on his way to meet you. When he sees you, he's going to be glad. You'll speak to him and tell him what to say. I'll be right there with you as you speak and with him as he speaks, teaching you step by step. He will speak to the people for you. He'll act as your mouth, but you'll decide what comes out of it. Now take this staff in your hand; you'll use it to do the signs." (Exodus 4:10-17 MSG).

The bible says God became angry with Moses. In another translation, it says God's anger kindled against Moses because Moses did not realize who he was. He focused so on his speech impediment resulting in him questioning himself because he feared rejection. Moses did not fully understand what or whom God placed on the inside of him. Nor did he realize who God was. Moses tried to convince Him that he was not the person for the assignment. God knew who Moses was because He created him. God said, "Look boy I know who you are and I know what I'm doing! I don't want to hear your excuses Moses!"

If you read the story of Moses, found in the book of Exodus, you will see how God manifested Himself through Moses. Despite how Moses felt God still performed many signs, miracles, and wonders and delivered the people out of hands of the enemy.

God placed His anointing inside of you at the time of conversion and places deposits of Himself (The anointing) inside you as you grow and mature and as He gives you assignments. His capabilities, abilities, and power are within you. Embrace the God on the inside of you. If you do, you will accomplish great things for the Kingdom.

The Anointing and YOU

God's manifested presence ties into knowing who you are. What does that mean? Well, let's just say God wants to use you to heal someone, but you don't know you can heal, or God wants to speak to someone through you, but you don't realize you have the gift of knowledge. To operate in the anointing that is inside of you, you must know whom you are and what you are called to do. Trust the anointing inside of you. What are you anointed to do? Every believer has an anointing to do something in and for the kingdom.

Demonstrate the Anointing
Demonstration + Power + Presence = Anointing

"I was unsure of how to go about this, and felt totally inadequate—I was scared to death, if you want the truth of it—and so nothing I said could have impressed you or anyone else. But the Message came through anyway. God's Spirit and God's power did it, which made it clear that your life of faith is a response to God's power, not to some fancy mental or emotional footwork by me or anyone else."
(I Corinthians 2:3-5 MSG).

Over the past 12 years, God has used me to demonstrate visually who He is, using the arts. I have spent countless hours planning and preparing for productions, choreodramas, women conferences, Sunday services, and teen events. I allowed God to have His hand on and in everything despite what I thought to be inadequacies and my fears.. This includes everything from putting together choreography, rehearsals, choosing the right person for a part, teaching movement, and choice of colors, garments, and music, to caring for the soul of the artist. He keeps me on task and I do the assignments according to His plan. Just as He was there for Moses every step of the way, He is here for me and He is here for you. When it comes time for the team to minister, despite my fears God manifests Himself anyhow. The key element is spending quality time with the Lord. He shows up mightily bringing, healing, deliverance, salvation, and joy. Lives change undoubtedly through the manifested presence of God.

The Anointing in a Corporate Setting
In my experience with Gods manifested presence I discovered unity is one of the key elements to what causes the anointing

to flow in a corporate setting. Creating an atmosphere where God is welcomed and the Holy Spirit can move is possible. The anointing (God's manifested presence) is conducive to the atmosphere which we create. Unity and oneness of mind, and focusing on God in one accord allows God to dwell in the midst of His people. God moves miraculously and simultaneously bringing about a manifested change.

The anointing exists in unity. The manifested results will be miracles, healings, deliverance, signs, and wonders, limbs growing, wounded hearts healed, disease and sickness destroyed, minds set free, and hearts changed.

> [1]*"Behold, how good and how pleasant it is for brethren to dwell together in unity! [2]It is like the precious ointment upon the head, that ran down upon the beard, even Aaron's beard: that went down to the skirts of his garments; [3]As the dew of Hermon, and as the dew that descended upon the mountains of Zion: for there the LORD commanded the blessing, even life for evermore." (Psalm 133:1-3 KJV).*

> [4-6]*"You were all called to travel on the same road and in the same direction, so stay together, both outwardly and inwardly. You have one Master, one faith, one baptism, one God and Father of all, who rules over all, works through all, and is present in all. Everything you are and think and do is permeated with Oneness." (Ephesians 4:4-6 MSG).*

In my heart I believe God should manifest in every service, the atmosphere should shift, and change should occur. There should be some sort of evidence that God is in the house. I was standing where I usually stand in church, doing what I usually do. Apostle Overton began to invite God into the atmosphere with the words of his mouth" Lord you are welcome here!" "We invoke the prophetic God!", "Come in and have your way Lord!" It was during praise and worship when the atmosphere began to shift.

The worship leader was ministering in song and I said to the Lord," that really sounds nice," so I began to sing along. Prophet

Overton said, "Someone else has the rest of the song." I found myself walking confidently and speedily to the front because I know who I am, and I know what God placed on the inside of me. I did not hear God say go to the front. I didn't feel anything when I was walking, it was just a knowing on the inside. When handed the microphone I started singing. However, IT WASN'T ME SINGING, it was God using my mouth, vocal cords, and my willingness to sing. I could feel the very presence of God in my belly. As I sang, I felt the depths God. I felt Him. It was so strong. It was if He was coming out through me and He was. It felt as though EVERYTHING stood still and He was the only one moving. He had something to say to His people. My God, it was the anointing! It was the manifested presence of God! That day people were set free from striving and from dead works because we were all of one mind, unified focused on God the Father.

    The remainder of the service and after I arrived home, I could still feel God in my belly. Through this experience and countless others what I found to be true is the anointing (the manifested presence of God) can come at any time. I did not do anything special. I was willing and obedient. I was just being whom God called and created me to be.

    It is that simple, be who God called you to be so His manifested presence is seen and felt through you. God is appealing and God is revealing through His anointing. We do not look for the anointing we are the anointing (as quoted by – Apostle Lawrence Overton)

About The Author

Deborah Settles

Deborah serves with a prophetic call on her life to destroy the works of the enemy through movement and the power of God's Word. Deborah is an anointed and prolific teacher as well as a choreographer. She is filled with God's power and ability to destroy the works of the enemy. She is a worship warrior and intercessor on behalf God's people and the nations. Deborah has a passion for the Kingdom of God and His people and a love for His Word.

Deborah was born in a small rural town in Trafford, Pennsylvania. She is number 7 of 8 children and encountered God at the age of 9. She rededicated her life to the Lord at the age of 21 and has been walking faithfully with the Lord for the past 25 years. She is a woman of integrity and compassion.

Deborah started her adult journey with the Lord by leading Sunday morning congregational prayer for thousands and was involved in weekly bible studies. Deborah served as an usher and sang in the full gospel Choir. For 6 years, Deborah remained at Mt. Ararat Baptist Church under the direction of Bishop Donald Clay. During her attendance she discovered her gifting and callings and a passion for prayer and intercessory. Also at this time, Deborah discovered she had a prophetic call on her life. Although she operated in the gifting, she did not fully understand. She simply lived the prophetic call. It was who she was and still is today. God continues to speak to Deborah through dreams, visions, and words about His people and the nations.

Since that time, Deborah has been involved with The Women's Intercessory Network, founded by Pastor Lorraine Williams. A network of women who have recognized the call of God in their lives to intercessory prayer and have therefore, committed themselves to that call. A ministry that brings intercessors together in unified prayer efforts to tear down the strongholds of the enemy in our cities, nation, and the world; as well as, our churches and families. Deborah became involved with Bridges of Hope, a ministry for unwed mothers. She has mentored single moms to help bring them to a place of confidence and reliance on God. Deborah attended a four-year program at Living Faith Training Center. Where the word of God was taught and His principles lived out. Her passion and calling lies in Worship arts and for the past 12 years Deborah has raised up countless teenagers, developing dancers and dramatist for the glory of the Lord.

As her walk with God grows and intensifies Deborah's passion and love for Christ grows. While out in the community, Deborah uses every opportunity to lay hands on the sick and to speak and pray into the lives of everyday people.

Deborah is a mother of three daughters and five grandchildren. She is the Managing Partner of Rever Designs, a web design and web development company. Soon to be birthed, Deborah and Company, a Worship Arts Center and the book The Definitive Work of Art - A Guide to the Art of Dance. Deborah currently resides in Arlington, VA and attends Kingdom Way International Ministries under the direction of Apostle Lawrence Overton and Prophet Felicia Overton.

If you are a single mom I have been there, if you have been divorced, I've been there, if you have a child on drugs, I've been there, if you were molested as a child, I've been there, if you are married to a drug addict, I've been there, if you were abandoned and raised yourself, I've been there, if you have a child who's on their death bed I've been there, if you experienced an abortion, I've been there, If you are young teen mom, I've been there, if you have been homeless, I've been there, If your without a job, I've been there. If your heart has been broken, I've been there. The pains that I have experienced have made me who I am today. Job 38:22 reads: have you entered the treasury of snow or have you seen the treasury of hail, which I HAVE RESERVED for the time of trouble for the day of battle & war. God has reserved the difficulties and the trials we face in life for us. The bible says God reserved these times just for us. These unique seasons were created to fit me. It was made just for me. God knew I could handle it. Because all that I have endured I am more than a conquer through Christ Jesus. There is nothing that God and I can't handle together!

Chapter 6

Be Free

The song that first appeared in my spirit when I heard the title to my chapter was "Born Free" by Andy Williams. I asked "Why this song Lord?" I went on a journey to find out why the Holy Spirit would sing this song to me. The words to this song are

"Born free", as free as the wind blows, As free as the grass grows, Born free to follow your heart, Stay free, where no walls divide you, You're free as the roaring tide, So there's no need to hide, Born free, and life is worth living, But only worth living, 'cause you're born free."

"Born Free" was the title to the movie and the theme song, based upon a maturing lion cub being re-educated to return to the wild and live free. I caught hold to this one word, re-educated. Originally, the cub was born in captivity. However, it was now approaching a defining moment: freedom. I could imagine the lion cub being somewhat used to its master telling him when he was going to be fed, when it would be brought to and from the cage and not knowing instinctively how to catch the food himself. The cub did not know what freedom was or what it meant to his animalistic survival skills. Captivity in a cage was not the way it should have been. Thus, the lyrics to the song help us to understand our topic today. Do you really understand the freedom that you possess through the saving blood of Jesus Christ? Let us explore.

Be Free, my title and assignment, is speaking to every Christian to take the liberty, that Jesus Christ paid for with His blood, and LIVE. This one act of love opens the door for every person to have access to God Jehovah. This one act of love brings us back into relationship with God, the relationship that Adam and Eve gave up in the Garden of Eden. Jesus' life, death, and resurrection provide us with an eternal and spiritual freedom from here to glory. *"For God so loved the world, that he gave his only begotten Son, that whosoever believeth in him should not perish, but have everlasting life."* (John 3:16 KJV). The enemy of our soul has a wicked agenda *"The thief cometh not, but for to steal, and to kill, and to destroy: I am come that they might have life, and that they might have [it] more abundantly."* (John 10:10 KJV) Our life is all we have in this world. Why would the God of the Heavens not want us to enjoy it?

Before I get started, I love sharing quotes. One of the most powerful statements for many social and political movements has been repeated, "Give me liberty or give me death" and was penned by Patrick Henry (1736 – 1799) an orator and politician who led the movement for independence in Virginia in the 1770s. The full quote is "Is life so dear, or peace so sweet, as to be purchased at the price of chains and slavery? Forbid it, Almighty God! I know not what course others may take; but as for me, give me Liberty, or give me Death!"

Christ paid for our liberty, our freedom from sin and death. *"For ye are bought with a price: therefore glorify God in your body, and in your spirit, which are God's."* (1 Corinthians 6:20 KJV). The price that God paid was the blood of His own Son. We read in Romans 6:18 (KJV) *"Being then made free from sin, ye became the servants of righteousness."* Now we need to take bold steps in keeping our freedom and not going back to our former slave master, sin. We are no longer bound to the yokes of sin that had us chained to an eternal destiny of doom and loss of contact with the Creator, Jehovah. Our new Master and Savior, only wants good for us. Now we must serve God through righteous living in His kingdom. This heavenly and spiritual kingdom is established with its rules, regulations, and policies. Where can we find them? Can they be found? They are found in the holy word of God, the Bible. Are you willing to do the research and take the journey in the word to search out the principles of this kingdom? In the natural sense, each kingdom has a king. The king has set up a kingdom with certain rules. The United States has a president. I reside in the United States and have pledged my allegiance to the flag for which it stands. The rules, regulations of the land I reside determine my natural freedom.

How bad do you want your freedom in the spiritual kingdom? Most recently on my weekly radio show, Holy Nation of Women, Pastor Shirley Bryant interjected on our topic "My Liberty." Pastor Bryant read that Mrs. Harriet Tubman was a fearless and tireless leader. Mrs. Tubman was the Underground Railroad leader who fought for and delivered many lives through the doors of freedom. She was not a woman to play with. She was serious about the cause of letting her people out of the hands of a brutal slave master. She did not just free herself from a life of slavery but others counted on her bravery to lead them, to fight and outwit a determined enemy. For those who were not as tough as she was, my mother read this passage to help us understand our topic for the show: "For the faint of heart she carried a pistol, telling her charges to go on or die, for a dead fugitive slave could tell no tales."

I said in response to this reading that this was one tough woman. Mrs. Tubman was not going to let a weak and scared slave ruin everyone else's chance for freedom. They were leaving the south and headed north to the promise of freedom to those who made it. My family, whether they know it or not, need me to be strong, vigilant and determined, fighting the good fight of faith. Mrs. Tubman definitely inspires me to be strong and courageous. I will continue to ask myself this question as I face new challenges. Can I, and will I stand for my freedom at all cost? *"Finally, my brethren, be strong in the Lord, and in the power of his might." (Ephesians 6:10 KJV). Are you scared? 4"For whatsoever is born of God overcometh the world: and this is the victory that overcometh the world, [even] our faith. 5Who is he that overcometh the world, but he that believeth that Jesus is the Son of God?" (I John 5:4-5 KJV).* My dear sisters and brothers, are you free today? Are you completely living out the liberty that is so freely yours? Are you sold out to the very end? Will you make it? Are you completely convinced?

As we read further in Romans, Paul is so convincingly correct in his statements; that we are no slaves to the power of this flesh if we have been born again. Born into a new kingdom, where the King of Kings is Jesus Christ, the son of God, where Christ has dominion. This new kingdom has a different set of rules, regulations, and policies – including the freedom purchased by the blood of Jesus Christ. All power belongs to Our Lord and Savior Jesus Christ. The keys to death and the grave were stripped from our former slave master, Satan. He no longer has holds on us other than what we give him. That relationship is over, dead.

[11]"Likewise reckon ye also yourselves to be dead indeed unto sin, but alive unto God through Jesus Christ our Lord. [12]Let not sin therefore reign in your mortal body, that ye should obey it in the lusts thereof. [13]Neither yield ye your members [as] instruments of unrighteousness unto sin: but yield yourselves unto God, as those that are alive from the dead, and your members [as] instruments of righteousness unto God." (Romans 6:11-13 KJV).

Looking at verse 12, we see that the key word for us is "reign." Who is in charge of your comings and goings? Are you trying to deceive God and have a silent partner advising you as well? Sin will reign if you let it. Sin is deceptive and if you play both sides of the fence God states in his word that he will have nothing to do with you if you will not make the choice. *"So then because thou art lukewarm, and neither cold nor hot, I will spew thee out of my mouth."* (Revelations 3:16 KJV). Why would you want to play with the evil one knowing his one ultimate goal is to steal, kill, and destroy the saints of God? You are his number one enemy. The devil has his fate determined and if he can get indecisive saints to sway back and forth in their belief in the all-powerful God then Satan will make you pay for turning away from Him. The choice is yours in following God's precepts and concepts in His word. The question to consider: Do you really believe the Jesus has the power to help you?

Romans 6 verse 13 states, "neither yield ye your members." In other words, do not take yourself back to the enemy of your soul and entangle yourself with the deeds of unrighteousness; or give yourself over to lusts and temptations of your former slave master, which is certain death, spiritual death. *"Who shall separate us from the love of Christ? [shall] tribulation, or distress, or persecution, or famine, or nakedness, or peril, or sword?"* (Romans 8:35 KJV).

Harriet Tubman knew that the fate of a returning slave was a beating and enslavement upon reentry into the plantation. Mrs. Tubman was going to take the slaves out of their misery for making the wrong choice, and the possibility of endangering other lives. Bravery and courage seemed to be a running slave's only option. Freedom was their destiny but the slave would have to make a decision to follow Mrs. Tubman with complete trust in her ability to take them on this journey.

You are free to live and obey what is right. Are you brave enough to tell your flesh that you will not cooperate in its call for your return to sin? Are you courageous enough, in the midnight hour of despair, to wait on the Lord to bring you victory? Will you endure hardness (tribulations, tests, trials) as a good soldier, give me liberty, or give me death? Will you submit yourself to the Father's way? Last of all will you BE FREE in the new dominion of Christ Jesus. We are in the world, but not of the world. There are many temptations to fight against but there is a way that is better than what our human flesh demands.

The power of God is in us to live right. It is a journey to the "promised land." The journey takes time. It was not an overnight process once the slave fled the old master. They followed the leader through treacherous nights to the "underground" hidings, with fearful conviction. One day at a time, they were free - disconnected from the evil one and the plantation. "I'm free," was a thought that was truer every step of the way.

What happens when you step over to unbelief and sin? *"For the wages of sin [is] death; but the gift of God [is] eternal life through Jesus Christ our Lord."* (Romans 6:23 KJV). Paul clearly shows that there is a reward for either choice. Why get a payday for a sinful life? Sin has its mark and reward for the one who wants or returns to a life of sin. The slave wore the clothing of the slave master, the brand, the beating, and the demolition of their humanity.

The freed men and women were now on the road of freedom looking for a new name, new city, new friends, new homes, and new situations all with fear of the unknown. In this new life the slave would drop his old nametag and would be free to do as he pleased and live without shame and humiliation. They would be free to live out in the open in the new land in the North to prosper, sing, enjoy, work, and raise a family by starting anew in this new kingdom.

You, as a Christian, are born into a spiritual kingdom. The Book of Matthew clearly tells of God's care and of this new kingdom in the gospel account of Jesus' words on the mountain.

[30]"Wherefore, if God so clothe the grass of the field, which today is, and tomorrow is cast into the oven, [shall he] not much more [clothe] you, O ye of little faith? [31]Therefore take no thought, saying, What shall we eat? or, What shall we drink? or, Wherewithal shall we be clothed? [32](For after all these things do the Gentiles seek:) for your heavenly Father knoweth that ye have need of all these things. [33]But seek ye first the kingdom of God, and his righteousness; and all these things shall be added unto you." (Matthew 6:30-33 KJV).

What are the things that we put before our relationship with God? Do not let yourself end up in a sinful state because you figured out how to get stuff. Do not be tied up with the yokes of bondage or the world's entanglements by letting stuff get a hold of you.

Harriet Tubman was a Moses. Moses was a very popular name during this time. In searching for my mother's great- great-grandfather I discovered his first name was Morris. I thank God for this, for every other male child was Moses and I would not have found my grandfather in the archives. Mrs. Tubman knew of the story of deliverer called Moses and the significance it had to her people. She could identify with the story and the people who had to suffer at the hands of cruelty. Mrs. Tubman had a plan and worked her plan, successfully, freeing slaves one by one. She intervened when she could have just saved herself and family. Without any fear, she was determined to go back in the darkest of night to sneak out hundreds to their freedom repeatedly.

Are you leading anyone out of bondage from the master called sin? Are you snatching someone from the jaws of hell, death, and destruction, going on undercover missions, late night prayer vigils, and intercessory tag teams?

As I close, another scripture that comes to mind *"Now the Lord is that Spirit: and where the Spirit of the Lord [is], there [is] liberty."* (II Chronicles 3:17 KJV). The wind has liberty to blow at will and in any direction. The waves ask "how high today?" The grass bursts forth her shoots to look for more rain and sun. God who considers you more than these is telling you today to BE FREE in His Kingdom where He reigns. You do not have to die to get there. It is available right now. Walk in it, live in it, realize it, and rest in the freedom and liberty of Christ Jesus. Christ rose on the third day after his crucifixion and paved the way for you to enjoy the kingdom now. Through His suffering, He knows all you are going through in this evil world. He knew that you would need someone to help you. The Comforter resides in you, leading you, and guiding you to all truths. There is no need to fret or worry. He is going to talk to you, sing to you, and whisper his love to you in the midnight hour as you travel on this life's journey. Know this with absolute surety. If you have Jesus as your personal savior, you have the Holy Spirit, which is the Comforter, Jesus the Son, and God the Father rooting for you. They know the way to the Promised Land if you allow them to lead you. *"If the Son therefore shall make you free, ye shall be free indeed."* (John 8:36 KJV).

Is Christ Jesus in your heart today? Has He made a permanent and indelible mark on your heart? If not, He is still waiting for that true yes.

About The Author

Beverly Goodwin

Beverly Goodwin is the CEO of Holy Nation of Women. She gave her life to Jesus Christ at the age of 13 at Peoples Christian Church of Deliverance where Arthur S Conward was the Pastor. Evangelist Beverly received the baptism of the Holy Ghost when she was 24, the night before she would become deathly ill. She did not succumb to the sickness because of God's prevailing hand in her life. In 2001, she became an ordained minister while serving under Pastor Robert Conward, St James Restoration ACCG. She is now serving under the leadership of his brother, Pastor Russell Conward, Faith International Church, where she was ordained an evangelist in July 2007. She has served as Choir Member, Sunday School Teacher, Missionary, and Praise and Worship Team Member.

March 2009 was the revival of the ministry God had given her in 2002, Holy Nation of Women, which is covered by Pastor Tammy McNair of Sister Circle Ministries. Evangelist Beverly released a book entitled "Let's Take Our Devotion to Another Level" in December 2010. She now hosts a weekly radio show, on Blogtalkradio.com, discussing the devotions in the book. Evangelist Beverly endeavors to keep the ministry going through God Jehovah's help and goes out into the community doing outreach ministry to the unsaved. Her mission is 2 Chronicles 7:14, to help women to hear from God and heal their land through neighborhood outreaches, bible studies, and prayer vigils. She has been married to Kevin Goodwin for 28 years, has 4 beautiful children, LyAvia, Kellen, Katrina and Kavita, and two grandchildren, Leilani and Lauren.

www.holynationofwomen.org

Chapter 7

Bought With A Price

"The LORD is my shepherd; I shall not want." (Psalm 23:1 KJV).

When you become a follower of Jesus Christ there is a hefty price to pay. God requires you to reject yourself and take on a life conducive to Christ.

Treasures after Tragedies (The "Give Up" Moment)

The past four years have been a rough & bumpy road for me. God allowed me to have a Job like experience. At the beginning stages of my endurance challenge, I knew of Christ yet I did not have an intimate (personal) relationship with Him. All within the same year, I lost my cousin, my home, and my vehicle.

I was OFFICALLY done with life. I was at a point of hopelessness. Death's door was my way out. It became my best friend. There was no life left in me. My cousin was shot and killed one month, I lost my home the next month, and then to add more pain to my situation, I lost my vehicle at the end of that year. Through it all God still covered me. When you become part of the royal family, you will experience some grave times in your life but your Father who loves and adores you will protect His children. The enemy's plan is to get you to say what you see. The bible says, *"Faith without works is dead."* (James 2:17 KJV). Put faith to work! Do not proclaim what your situation says hear the voice of God and apply that to your situation.

The Price...

"Wisdom is the principal thing; therefore get wisdom: and with all thy getting get understanding." (Proverbs 4:7 KJV).

My desire was to give up before I had the chance to win. I figured since lost it ALL, I must be good at it. My professional status was losing. Even in your losing moments, God certainly has not forgotten about you. It amazes me when the price to pay is at an all-time high, we, as human beings tend to give up the most. However, when the cost is less or none at all, people will stand in line for days. We will take on some extreme weather conditions just to get what we want. Take on that same approach and apply it to paying the price for being a child of the Most High God. For me at first I did not understand the logic of going through for Christ. If God is God then why should I have to struggle? Then God revealed to me struggle has its purpose and you must go through the process. With everything, comes process.

Process is the evitable. You cannot get around nor can you get away from it. It took thirty years for Jesus to debut the earth with His ministry. Just imagine what God was doing with the first thirty years of Jesus' life. I believe God allowed Jesus to go through the process. Had He not gone through the process He would not have made it to the cross. I wish things could work out in rapid timing. Lord knows some of things I see in my life today would be gone tomorrow. A little secret I want to share with you that God gave to me is those things that require stamina remains as a plague in your life, and those things God sees as a threat to the promise must go. God's heart desire is to see you reach across the finish line. Your life means just that much to Jesus. It is an honor & a privilege to have our debt (sin) paid in full, the Price!!!

The Misconception...

"Those who control their tongue will have a long life; opening your mouth can ruin everything." (Proverbs 13:3 NLT).

In view of the fact that the world was on my shoulders, I felt why not take that plunge and just drown in my distress and mess. I was in disarray mentally, emotionally and physically. My life was a poignant roller coaster. I just existed. I hated myself. There was a mask that I had been wearing called the mask of "shame." I was so ashamed of myself that I begin to shut out all of my family and friends. My marriage was on the rocks. It was devastating. The enemy trapped me within my mind. I could not see past what I was going through. Lord knows, I just wanted to crawl in a cave and die. I truly hated what I had done to get to that point in my life. Fear came upon me. I became fearful of everything. Fear and shame grabbed hold of me. To top it off, that next year two more of my cousins were killed, and two of my aunts died as well. The following year, my dad passed. To talk about tragedy you had to have gone through it enough to be able to identify with it.

It is not an easy job to deal with God. Furthermore, only God can equip you to go through which I do not take it lightly. I know now that God's desire is to use me in such a way that even I cannot began to sum it all up. Satan wanted me to misunderstand what God was doing in my life. My life was lived out through tunnel vision. To continue on this great walk with God you must change your direction and vocabulary. Stop saying things that do not associate with the Kingdom of God. God's word speaks the truth. My mindset began to change. Instead of operating on what I see factor I started working off the TRUST FACTOR. No matter what comes my way, I will trust God! My motto now is do not beat yourself up. Rather, live with the things you could not accomplish. If God gives you grace to do those things over by all means do so. However, do not continue to beat yourself up just because you could not fulfill those things. Just maybe it was not in the plan of God anyway.

God's Plan...

"So God created man in his own image, in the image of God created he him; male and female created he them." Genesis 1:27 (KJV).

This portion was challenging to write. Day by day, I would get stuff and then revise it over again. Then God said to me "Do you really know the plan I have for you"? Lord what is my strategy? When you go through it tends to keep you from seeing God's plan for your life. At first, I could not understand why God allowed me to lose people, things, and even myself in all of this. Nonetheless, God's plans are personalized and thought-out carefully for our lives. He knows just when to go about a thing. When He allows certain things to take place in your life you experience first- hand the power of God. Going through is not intended to harm you in any way. It may seem like a set-up by God when in fact it is a set apart so God can get the glory out of it. We fail to believe that when faced with a crisis it is in the plan of God. When just like Job, God allows us to be broken so that we can see those things holistically through the lens of God.

I know life can hurt. Yes, you want to give up. Please do not think you are the only one going through. Allow me to clarify the myth…you are not the only one. Every seasoned Christian has challenging moments. There is no PERFECTION in this Christian walk. Daily, we have to die to self. We all are sinners saved by grace. Do not miss the move of God by having a cloudy vision. Sit at His feet and be attentive to the voice of God. My situation paralyzed me from hearing the voice of God. The belief system that I had has moved to the back of the line. My mind had me believing that God did not care about me. The life that He gave to me was so messed up I could not find the end from the beginning. When you are' out of touched with God, it is hard to understand His plan and purpose for your life. That is why relationships where designed. The most profound relationship God gave to us is marriage. It displays the core values God intended between the church and Him. If you find yourself in a place where you are not able to hear from God create a space where you can hear God. Yes, you may have gone astray but just like that old saying, "you are never too old to get an education," the same method applies to coming back to God.

The "Bounce-Back" Queen…

"The LORD shall preserve thee from all evil: he shall preserve thy soul. The LORD shall preserve thy going out and thy coming in from this time forth, and even for evermore." (Psalm 121:7-8 KJV).

What is the point in still holding? What is accomplishable by remaining as a true believer of Christ? Knowing the Lord became an assignment to me. I desired to know God even more in my mess. Although, I have not been physically delivered from those tragedies as of yet, my soul is well with what I have gone though. I now have a clearer picture of what God is doing in my life. There is a call on my life and with that call comes much longsuffering and determination on my part. Daily, I deny myself for the cause. I am now able to put my past into words. God's word is what sustains me in every trial, tribulation, persecution, pain, and hurt I endure. I travel with the word of God. I even have the word of God hidden in my heart. The word of God was necessary back then and the word of God is still necessary in this day and time. To live a life patterned after Christ you must bear the cross. Once you have done away with self then Christ can reign and rule in your life. It is called "access granted" a right to entry. Initially, I had no idea that all God wanted was entry. He seeks after His investment. God wanted to start the birthing process in me.

Since I was shameful and felt guilty of my past, I just knew I could not hold up my end. On many occasions, I said to God that I could not do it. I wanted to end it all. I was depressed, confused and had a lot of hurt bottled down on the inside of me. The enemy had me living within the walls of my mind. It ruled me and my mind was doing some crazy things to me. Waking up for work was challenging because I felt depleted and down. The enemy had me right where he wanted me. Until one day, I began to live again. I saw that I was not the only one living this life. The bible says, **"Greater is He that's within me than he that's within the world"** (I John 4:4 KJV). God provided me with his help. At that very moment, I knew there must be a God! The Lord showed up and showed out in my life.

If I never reach that point in my life, where those things I have lost are returned to me I believe I am far better off now than where I was. By going through, I understand it was for my good. I have obtained Kingdom Citizenship, in this world but not of the world. I acknowledge that although the reward for kingdom citizenship is great the cost is even greater. Kingdom Citizenship is when you do away with the old way of living (sinful life) and you take on a new life in Christ by becoming a citizen of the Kingdom (heaven bound). From tragedies to treasures is the day the Bounce-Back Queen was born!

About The Author

Kisha L. Campbell

Kisha L. Campbell is a native Washingtonian, born to the late Anthony Moten Sr. and Vanette Moten. She is the eldest of four children. Kisha attended and completed her educational years of training in the District of Columbia Public School System. At the tender age of twelve Kisha accepted the Lord and Saviour Jesus Christ into her life under the Senior Pastorship of the Late Bishop Henry Williams. As a young child, Kisha loved to sing and be a part of the Youth Church Ministries.

In 1997, she joined Lively Stone Worship Center (currently Kingdom Harvest Ministries) where the Senior Pastor is District Elder Floyd E. Nelson II in Landover, MD. Her heart is one for reaching out and touching those who have experienced great loss and destitution. She functions as the Vice President to the Outreach Ministry where she passionately touches those who are lost. She serves as a Councilman for a Company of Intercessors called The Prophetic Intercessors Council of an Empowered People (PICEP). Her mission is to see God's people empowered, by educating them in God's word, which equips them to be strong soldiers' for Christ. Kisha is currently pursuing a Bachelor's Degree in Business with Capella University. She is employed with the Department of Justice as a legal assistant. Kisha is a faithful and loving wife to Nathan Campbell Jr. Together they have six beautiful children, four sons and two daughters.

Kisha's signature scripture is Psalm 107:20 KJV **"He sent his word, and healed them, and delivered them from their destructions."**

Chapter 8

Before The Fall
(God's Original Design)

²⁶"And God said, Let us make man in our image, after our likeness: and let them have dominion over the fish of the sea, and over the fowl of the air, and over the cattle, and over all the earth, and over every creeping thing that creepeth upon the earth. ²⁷So God created man in his own image, in the image of God created he him; male and female created he them. ²⁸And God blessed them, and God said unto them, Be fruitful, and multiply, and replenish the earth, and subdue it: and have dominion over the fish of the sea, and over the fowl of the air, and over every living thing that moveth upon the earth." Genesis 1:26-28 (KJV).

I first want to thank God for the opportunity to be a part of such an awesome project. I pray that my part in this endeavor will please Almighty God as I take part in the vision that God has given Overseer Trena Stephenson. It is my prayer that you will be spiritually equipped, transformed, and restored to God's Original Design after reading this selection.

Daily I rise and give God glory for the day. As a prayer leader on a 7 days a week prayer line, I have the privilege of offering the first fruit of the day to God with a group of awesome intercessors (prayer warriors). We teach the word as well as take prayer request from those online. We pray about any of the life circumstances that any or all of us may face. This could be marriages, finances, businesses, occupations, ministries, health etc. Whatever it is, we pray. We come together believing that whatsoever we petition God for, it shall happen.

We have received so many testimonies about the goodness of the Lord, about healing, deliverance, and provision that only He could do. Still somehow, some way we all have felt that there was more to this than meets the eye. I could tell you what the word says about the miracles, signs, and wonders. I know whatever we bind on earth is bound in heaven and whatever we loose on earth is loosed in heaven, but God something is still missing.

The believer is still dying of cancer. The believer is still out of work and facing foreclosure. The believer is still struggling with all kinds of addictions, i.e., drugs, pornography, food, and sex. Divorce is at 50% amongst Christians. Father, what is it? What are we missing?

The world has more access to the word than ever before yet it seems like we are worse off than ever. The church looks like and acts like the world. Our music is so similar to the secular that clubs can play it, and the world can dance to it. We cannot tell them apart. The unsaved do not see enough holiness in the saved to compel them to repentance asking; "what must I do to be saved?"

The saved, sanctified body of Christ is crying out for more. Why are we not casting out more demons? Why are we not operating in the supernatural? Why is healing not taking place just because they walked past my shadow? Is this the way you intended it to be from the very beginning?

Well after weeks of pondering and praying, God brought forth revelation. In other words, He began to reveal Himself and what His original plan. When it happened, I was on the prayer line and Prophet Timothy Silver was doing the teaching. When he began to speak, he was confirming some things that the Lord spoke to me while revealing others. I could have hollered. God you are so awesome, so amazing. Even though I was glad to hear the good news from the Lord and my brother in Christ, it brought me to a place of repentance. Lord I have missed this for so long. I knew what you said others and I were to walk in and do, but I just could not figure out how to accomplish it. Now I know. Truly as a man thinketh, so is he.

Beloved what God revealed should blow your mind. This revelation will let you know who you are and what God's intent was from the very beginning. This will set you free. Now walk with me through Genesis 1:26-28 and see/hear what the Lord is saying. Are you ready? Let me inform you that the definitions of several words are given. It is imperative that you receive the full meaning of the word in order to understand what God was saying.

Let us look at Genesis 1:26. *"And God said, Let us make man in our image, after our likeness: and let them have dominion over the fish of the sea, and over the fowl of the air, and over the cattle, and over all the earth, and over every creeping thing that creepeth upon the earth."* (KJV).

This statement was made on the 6th day of creation. After God had created everything else, He conferred with God the Son and God the Holy Spirit, saying, "Let us make man in our image." Stop right there. Let us define the word "image":

- Actual or mental picture: a picture or likeness of somebody or something, produced either physically by a sculptor, painter, or photographer, or formed in the mind
- Likeness seen or produced: the likeness of somebody or something that appears in a mirror, somebody closely resembling somebody else: a person or thing bearing a close likeness to somebody or something else "She's the image of her father."
- A very typical or extreme example of something
- Representation, illustration, reflection, picture, icon, figure, impression, copy, twin, double, duplicate, spitting image, carbon copy, appearance, look

Now hear what the Lord was saying. Let us reproduce ourselves. Let us make man our double. He created us to be a duplicate of Himself. He created us to be His twin, a carbon copy, or spitting image of Himself. He created us to mimic Him. Are you getting this? We are to be "like God"! He made us to resemble Him/

Them. He made us in His image. Say it aloud. You need to hear it. Repeat it. "I am made in the image of God. I am made in His likeness. He is my Father and I look like my daddy. Hallelujah!"

We are to do the things He did. When He made Adam and Eve, they were a carbon copy of Him. They were perfect and had perfect relationship with God and each other. They conversed with God whenever they chose. They had perfect spiritual communication. There was no sin, no arguments and no sickness. When God created everything else, He said "Let there be" and there was. We were created to do the same. Remember we are a carbon copy or mirror image of Him.

In verse 26 God then says *"and let them have dominion over the fish of the sea, and over the fowl of the air, and over the cattle, and over all the earth, and over every creeping thing that creepeth upon the earth."* After He made us in His image, He then gives mankind "dominion" over every living thing. So look at "dominion":
- Ruling control: ruling power, authority, or control
- Sphere of influence: somebody's area of influence or control
- Land ruled: the land governed by a ruler (often used in the plural)
- Say-so, domination, dominance, territory, colony, region, state, domain.

Do you see this? We are made in the image of God, perfectly spiritually communicating with Him. He gave man/us "dominion," ruling power, authority, control, and influence over every living thing. Understand that at this time, Adam was limitless in what he could do and think because he was "like" God. God's original intent was to communicate with us/man spiritually and not physically. Adam was complete within himself. In Adam was presence, purpose, provision, position, profession, and productivity. (Genesis1:26-29, Genesis 2:15-20).

Then in verse 28 *"And God blessed them, and God said unto them, Be fruitful, and multiply, and replenish the earth, and subdue it: and have dominion over the fish of the sea, and over the fowl of the* air, and over every living thing that moveth upon the earth." (Genesis 1:28 KJV).

God blesses mankind. What does it mean to "bless"?
- Make somebody or something holy: to bestow holiness on somebody or something in a religious ceremony
- Protect somebody or something: to watch over somebody or something protectively
- Wish somebody or something well: to declare approval and support for somebody or something
- Confer desirable quality on somebody: to give somebody a desirable quality or talent (usually passive)
- Thank somebody: to express heartfelt thanks to somebody
- To invoke divine favor upon.
- To confer well-being or prosperity on.
- To endow, as with talent.

God blesses them, makes them holy, protects, and watches over them. He invokes divine favor upon and confers well-being and prosperity upon them. He tells them to go forth, be fruitful, and multiply. First, Man is made in the image of God. Then God tells him to reproduce others that will also be in God's image. Now let us look at Genesis 3:1-6.

¹"Now the serpent was more subtle than any beast of the field which the LORD God had made. And he said unto the woman, Yea, hath God said, Ye shall not eat of every tree of the garden? ²And the woman said unto the serpent, We may eat of the fruit of the trees of the garden: ³But of the fruit of the tree which is in the midst of the garden, God hath said, Ye shall not eat of it, neither shall ye touch it, lest ye die. ⁴And the serpent said unto the woman, Ye shall not surely die: ⁵For God doth know that in the day ye eat thereof, then your eyes shall be opened, and ye shall be "as gods," knowing good and evil. ⁶And when the woman saw that the tree was good for food, and that it was pleasant to the eyes, and a tree to be desired to make one wise, she took of the fruit thereof, and did eat, and gave also unto her husband with her; and he did eat. (KJV).

Here we see Eve tempted by Satan. Temptation could only come by something from the outside because she was complete on the inside. This is the same way Satan tempted Jesus after 40 days of fasting. Satan offered Jesus what was already His. Jesus knew who He was and what was already His. He was not fooled. The difference here is that somehow Eve forgot who she was. She forgot she was already "like God," she was made in His image. Therefore she was tempted to eat the fruit so that she might be "like God," something that she already was. When she and Adam disobeyed God, what was once pure, perfect, limitless, now became limited as sin entered the world.

When God told Adam and Eve to go forth, be fruitful, and multiply, they were to replenish the earth with children made in "God's image." After sin came into play, man was reproduced after the fallen image of Adam and not God. We have lived a limited lifestyle ever since. It was as if this was the end of what God intended. Glory is to God, He made a way out for us.

"For GOD so loved the world that HE gave HIS only begotten Son that whoever believes in Him should not perish but have everlasting life." (John 3:16 KJV). That is right; Jesus' death and resurrection redeemed us and restored us to our original state. Now we can communicate with God spiritually. Now we can walk again in authority. We, in Jesus' name can lay hands on the sick and they shall recover. Demons will flee when in our presence because of the anointing of God, the power and the authority we now walk. We can bind things or loose things here on earth and it is the same in heaven.

The problem is that we have believed the lie of the deceiver and bought into it for so long, that even after redemption we still live a life full of limitations. Our thoughts limit our spiritual productivity. How big is the God you serve? Open your mind and realize that you/we serve a limitless God. He can be as big as you can imagine or as small as you think. I choose to believe that all things are possible with God without limits. I choose to believe that I am created in His image. Therefore, I can do all things through Christ who strengthens me. I believe that God's original intent was for his children to be like Him. We are to represent Him, mimic Him, and be the mirror image of Him. We are to operate in the supernatural so much so that it becomes natural to us. The world should see God in us. Only after we get the revelation of whom God really is can we come to know whom we really are. I am a chosen generation, a royal priesthood, a holy nation, a peculiar person; that I should show forth the praises of Him who hath called me out of darkness into His marvelous light. I am owned by and purchased with the blood of the lamb. If you believe in Jesus Christ our Lord and Savior then you too shall receive restoration to the original intent of God.

"And be not conformed to this world: but be ye transformed by the renewing of your mind, that ye may prove what is that good, and acceptable, and perfect, will of God." (Romans 12:2 KJV).

We must renew our minds so that we can operate in God's original intent, the perfect will of God. I am so excited about this newfound life, this revelation. I am excited about not just saying I am a child of God but really KNOWING it and walking in it. I expect miracles, healings, deliverance, salvation, restoration, and the like. I expect to spiritually flow in supernatural because my "Daddy" does and I am just like Him. Hallelujah.

God has blessed us with all spiritual blessings. He has chosen us before the foundation of the world. The mystery of His will is made known unto us.

[3]"Blessed be the God and Father of our Lord Jesus Christ, who hath blessed us with all spiritual blessings in heavenly places in Christ: [4]According as he hath chosen us in him before the foundation of the world, that we should be holy and without blame before him in love: [5]Having predestinated us unto the adoption of children by Jesus Christ to himself, according to the good pleasure of his will, [6]To the praise of the glory of his grace, wherein he hath made us accepted in the beloved. [7]In whom we have redemption through his blood, the forgiveness of sins, according to the riches of his grace; [8]Wherein he hath abounded toward us in all wisdom and prudence; [9]Having made known unto us the mystery of his will, according to his good pleasure which he hath purposed in himself: [10]That in the dispensation of the fullness of times he might gather together in one all things in Christ, both which are in heaven, and which are on earth; even in him:"

(Ephesians 1:3-10 KJV).

      Beloved, I encourage you to renew your mind far beyond the borders in which you now think and operate. Realize that because of our Lord and Savior, Jesus the Christ, we receive restoration into God's original design. We are made in His image and can operate in the fullness thereof. Be Blessed.

About The Author

Bishop Etta Banks

Bishop Etta Banks became an active member of The Spirit and the Bride Christian Fellowship under the leadership of Pastors Robert and Annette Stagmer in 1983. There, she faithfully served as trustee, member of the intercessory prayer team, Assistant Director of Women in Christ and Women in Crisis (WIC) support group, choir director, and President of the Parent Teacher's Association at their academy. In 1989, Bishop Banks attended The East Baltimore Deliverance Church, where she established herself in outreach ministry, visiting hospitals, nursing homes, and prisons. She was also a member of the Deliverance Team, The Board of Trustees, and she taught Bible studies and life skills to men in transition as Pastor of New Vision for Life Kingdom Builders (vibrantly located in Randallstown, Maryland), which she founded, . Her ministries also include Christopher's Place Employment Academy. In 1994, Bishop Banks was licensed and ordained, then appointed head of the Couples Ministry for East Baltimore Deliverance Church.

In January 2003, Bishop Banks was ordained and installed as pastor of New Vision for Life Kingdom Builders. The ministry includes men and women groups, youth department, Praise and Worship team, personal and family counseling, Children's Church, Priceless Princess Ministry, Young Single Adults, and many others.

Among her accolades are Evangelical Theological Seminary, Institute of Motivational Living-Certified Behavioral Counselor, Certified Gifts Assessment Counselor/Trainer, Certified Prison Ministry Counselor, Certified through H.A.N.D.S.' Mentorship Program, certified Member of American Association of Christian Counselors. Bishop Banks' covering is Apostle Winston & Pastor Jacqueline Trought of Centerville, Massachusetts. They pastor Covenant on the Rock Family Church in Hyannis & Providence town, Massachusetts.

It is the heartfelt desire of Bishop Banks to inspire, motivate, empower, provoke, and encourage others to reach their fullest potential. Bishop Banks, by the awesome guidance of the Holy Spirit, prays that those who meet her will acquire a "New Vision For Life." She has two daughters Danielle Eldridge and Damitra Hardy eight grandchildren and five great-grandchildren, all working in ministry.

Chapter 9

Awaiting Your Arrival

As far back as I can remember I have longed for purpose. I was desperate for my life to have meaning. Along this journey, I have endured hardships, opposition, obstacles, and disappointments that were significant to my spiritual development and growth. As a result, God granted me this opportunity to share with you. Included in this chapter is a portion of my testimony along with biblical examples and scriptures. I sincerely hope you will find renewed strength and encouragement. Whether you are considering salvation, newly saved, returning to Him, or maturing in Christ, Jesus is awaiting your arrival with open arms.

Awaiting

According to the Free Dictionary by Farlex (2011), await means to wait, especially with expectation. Synonyms for this term include expect and anticipate. The title of this chapter signifies an anticipated arrival. The question is who is waiting and whose arrival is expected? Instinctively, I thought "Oh awaiting the arrival of God!" Upon further consideration, I recognize the human expectation or anticipation of God indicates belief in the departure or nonexistence of God. However, the Bible tells us that God is, always was, and always will be. He is Jehovah-Shamah, He is There; He is present (**Ezekiel 48:35**). He is Alpha and Omega; the beginning and the end; the first and the last (**Revelations 22:13**). Therefore, who is awaiting the arrival of whom? My friends, God is eagerly expecting you.

In the Beginning

In Genesis 1:26-27 and 2:7 we read that God created man in His image and likeness. Man was God's companion, someone with whom He could share and love. Regrettably, man abandoned God for a false opportunity to be like God without ever recognizing the greatness already given to him. In realization of their fatal mistake, Adam and Eve hid. How often have we turned away from God for something or someone that appeared better? How often have we put God in a corner until we find ourselves in despair?

Shortly following the creation of man, humanity rejected God and has done so repeatedly, yet God has never abandoned us (**Hebrews 13:5**). In fact, God so loved the world that He sacrificed His only begotten son so that everyone who believes in Jesus can reconnect with God through the restoration of eternal life (**John 3:16**). Furthermore, God remains available to us throughout our moments of desperation. *"Fear thou not; for I am with thee: be not dismayed; for I am thy God: I will strengthen thee; yea, I will help thee; yea, I will uphold thee with the right hand of my righteousness"* (Isaiah 41:10 KJV).

The Journey

At the age of seven, I accepted Jesus as my personal savior and filled with the Holy Ghost that same year. Following that pivotal moment I found myself wondering, "Now what?" I struggled in church as a youth because the teachings were on holiness and salvation, but little explanation was given about activating spiritual gifts or developing a personal relationship with God. I did not know God's accessibility, nor did I understand my purpose in God's kingdom. During that same year, my parent's divorce was finalized. The aftermath of the divorce ignited a personal flame to help others avoid the pain unjustly inflicted upon my family.

In my teens, I remember sitting in my room talking to God

and reading my bible. It was also during this time that my father began a church in our home, and he gave me opportunity to become active in ministry. Around 13 or 14 the anointing to minister through singing, preaching, teaching, and helping others were undeniable. However, I felt trapped in an endless cycle of setbacks, disappointments, and wrong turns as I constantly fought for social acceptance and societal approval. I was in an identity crisis. I was like a pirate on a deserted island hopelessly searching for the proverbial X to mark the spot in which I would find the hidden treasure. ***"But we have this treasure in earthen vessels, that the excellency of the power may be of God, and not of us."*** (II Corinthians 4:7 KJV). I was like Adam and Eve; so close to God but did not know who I was in God. Even with the anointing of the Holy Ghost, I failed to exercise power (**Acts 1:8**) given by God to control my flesh. As a result, I behaved recklessly experimenting with alcohol; dancing at house parties and school dances; smoking cigarettes and cigars (on occasion); and flirting with boys. Even during that time, God's hedge was around me. The word of God says to count it all joy when we fall into diverse temptations (**James 1:2**). I am not happy about the choices I made, but I recognize this was part of my journey.

Shortly after graduating from high school, I became pregnant. At 18, I had no true direction for my life and was devastated. (Note: Pregnancy is the natural result of sexual intercourse. Ladies please remember God is the giver of life. Never think of your child as sin. Rather recognize your mistakes and confess the sin of fornication. Each child is indeed a gift from God.) Even after committing what I believed was the cardinal sin- fornication, God still loved me. I am not condoning teen pregnancy, but again this was my path.

Initially, I kept the pregnancy a secret from my father because I wanted to accept responsibility and make a life for my child and myself. I sought assistance through the government, which proved to be a humiliating and humbling experience. I remember sitting in a crowded waiting room filled with the stench of dirty diapers and the sound of crying babies. As I spoke with the caseworker, she pried into every aspect of my life. I no longer had the luxury of discretion or privacy. The promise of supposed free help controlled me. In my first trimester, I stayed sick, yet the state required that I attend a work program to find employment. God blessed. My first interview was successful, and I was hired. My supervisor showed compassion and understanding, as did the rest of the staff. They became family to me and nurtured me during the most difficult time in my life. My supervisor and coworkers drove me to the grocery store and back and forth to work.

At 19 and 6 ½ months pregnant, I moved into my first apartment. My stepbrother and mother provided me with furniture and the amenities. By the time my son was born, I was no longer on state assistance. Later, I moved into a two-bedroom townhouse and was blessed again with desires of my heart. A neighbor sold me living room furniture for $100. At age 20 God blessed me to purchase my first car for cash before obtaining my license. My stepfather and son's father (now husband) both taught me how to drive. Only one year later, I bought a brand new car. We serve a God who knows all. He is omniscient and as such has designed a specific path to lead each of His children directly back to His open arms. *"When my spirit was overwhelmed with me, then thou knewest my path"* (Psalms 142:3 KJV). It is only when we stray that we find ourselves in a state of bewilderment. Thus before making any move, we must acknowledge God in our ways so that He can direct our path (**Proverbs 3:6**). God can use any negative situation and turn it around for our benefit (**Romans 8:28**). As a single mother, I experienced the hand of God like never before. I watched in awe as He supplied my every need (**Philippians 4:19**). He proved to be Jehovah-Jireh (my provider).

In my early to mid-twenties, I embarked on a new adventure to pursue ministry! Fortunately, my Pastor allowed me to work in various areas of the church. Sometimes I questioned why I was to work in certain departments. However, I think my pastor was preparing me according to God's purpose for my life. In each facet of ministry assigned, I sought God for direction with the intent to support the Pastor's vision. While trying zealously to work in my calling I encountered rejection and persecution from brothers and sisters in Christ. Furthermore, some people were not receptive to my efforts or gifts because of I was a new member of the church. Some also discriminated my age and individualism. Having a background in music, I worked as a choir directress and praise and worship leader, but my technique was questioned. Then I organized the children's church and nursery ministries but did not receive adequate parental support. After completing training as a Sunday school teacher, I was perceived ill equipped to teach the age group assigned me. While working on the youth board, I did not fit in with the clique resulting in the rejection and ignoring of my ideas. Finally, I worked with the missionary department and felt embraced. I enjoyed the ministry of helping others. Unfortunately, confusion within the department limited the effectiveness.

During the trial of rejection, I saw faults, weaknesses, and insecurities within myself. God used these challenges to mold me; thus shaping my character for His work. He is the potter and I am the clay (Jeremiah 18:6). As a result, God taught me how to forgive others, extend grace, speak up, be orderly, and persevere. I learned humility; to control my anger (that was huge); obedience, and loyalty to God and leadership. God taught me to love myself. Thus, I learned to walk confidently in the gifts and calling given me by God. **I Peter 1:7 reads "That the trial of your faith, being much more precious than of gold that perisheth, though it be tried with fire, might be found unto praise and honour and glory at the appearing of Jesus Christ."** (KJV). Trials prepare us for our destiny in God.

Throughout life, I have endured experiences in which I questioned God's presence. I cried out; needing Him to show up in my life. While desperately searching for God, I never thought perhaps God was actually awaiting my arrival. After all, God is everywhere (omnipresent), at all times. Furthermore, God promised to never leave us nor forsake us; meaning He is always available and accessible to His children (**Hebrews 13:5**). Thus, the seeming delay in the anticipated arrival of God in my life and ministry is impossible according to *Philippians 1:6 "Being confident of this very thing, that he which hath begun a good work in you will perform it until the day of Jesus Christ"* (KJV). In actuality, sometimes delay is the process required to prepare us for ministry.

We Must Choose God

Even though God is always with us, there are instances when circumstances and sin cover us from His view. Jesus even endured the rejection of God when He bore the sins of humanity on the cross.

> *"And about the ninth hour Jesus cried with a loud voice, saying, Eli, Eli, lama sabachthani? that is to say, My God, my God, why hast thou forsaken me?"* (Matthew 27:46 KJV).

Just like the void, I felt when making bad choices in my teens, God cannot operate fully in nor commune totally with us when we are in sin. Often in the moment of transition is when we seek direction. In our moments of desperation, we seek answers. In moments of oppression, we seek relief. Unfortunately, it sometimes takes a significant move or breaking point to bring us to our knees. Then with shallow understanding fueled by self-righteous religious expectation of God, we maintain a sense of entitlement. In our finite minds, we expect the instantaneous move of God on our behalf even when we have not yet fulfilled what He has required of us.

Deuteronomy 28 speaks of the blessings promised to God's people. However, those blessings are conditional. God requires that we choose Him as our Lord, and savior. He wants to be there for us in every facet of our lives. He wants to take care of you. He loves us. Still, inheritance requires relationship. Some people are caught up in the promise but do not want to work or earn it. Later in Deuteronomy 28 are also the consequences if God's people decide not to follow His law. The opposite of a blessing is a curse. When we fail to choose God, we open ourselves up for further struggles and setbacks just like Adam and Eve did in the garden when they chose to listen to the serpent rather than God.

The Answer is on the Way

At this point, you are probably thinking over your journey and analyzing the choices you have made. You are currently in position to make some changes and prepare for His Arrival. I know you are saying, "Wait a minute! You said God is awaiting our arrival!" Yes, I did, but there are instances in which there is a delay in the move of God not because of lack of power on His part and not because of you. In actuality, spirits and principalities with the assignment to delay the move of God exist. Unfortunately, when

Adam and Eve sinned they gave control of this earth back to the devil. As a result, sometimes there is a delay in our blessings, but they are not denied. For 21 days, Daniel prayed and fasted on behalf of the people of Jerusalem and he thought his prayers went unanswered until suddenly one day an angel appeared.

"Then said he unto me, Fear not, Daniel: for from the first day that thou didst set thine heart to understand and to chasten thyself before thy God, thy words were heard, and I am come for thy words. [12] But the prince of the kingdom of Persia withstood me one and twenty days: but, lo, Michael, one of the chief princes, came to help me; and I remained there with the kings of Persia."[13] (Daniel 10:12-13 KJV).

Satan hopes that if he delays your blessings that you will make a mistake and turn your back on God. Have you ever felt you were complete in one area? Suddenly the same test comes again, and you slip up leaving you with shame and guilt. *"For the good that I would I do not: but the evil which I would not, that I do"* (Romans 7:19 KJV). I want to encourage you today. If you are lining up with God's word and are diligently seeking Him but still He seems distant and your prayers unanswered, God already heard you. *"For I am persuaded, that neither death, nor life, nor angels, nor principalities, nor powers, nor things present, nor things to come, nor height, nor depth, nor any other creature, shall be able to separate us from the love of God, which is in Christ Jesus our Lord."* (Romans 8:38-39 KJV).

Conclusion

Every person is on this earth for a purpose. Each individual has the choice to pursue the designated destiny as assigned by God or to stray in the opposite direction. *"Choose you this day who ye will serve"* (Joshua 24:15 KJV). Understanding the mysteries of God through human reasoning is impossible. We fear God has distanced himself from our cares and struggles, but *"God is our refuge and strength, a very present help in times of trouble"* (Psalms 46:1 KJV). He will never leave us nor forsake us (**Hebrews 13:5**). In order for His promises to become active in our lives, we must follow His commandments whole-heartedly and make Him Lord of our lives. We must become one with Him (God) by accepting Jesus into our hearts and embracing the Holy Spirit.

      Friends, do not think that God has ever walked away from you. Even in those late hours as you sit alone, restless, and overwhelmed; God is Jehovah-Shamah (He is there). Even though we sometimes choose to stray from His divine path in search of satisfaction; he already made a way for our return to Him through the selfless sacrifice of His son Jesus (**John 3:16**). In actuality, since the fall of Adam and Eve, God has been patiently awaiting *your* arrival into His loving arms.

About The Author

Minister Renatta Jones-Brice

Minister Renatta Jones-Brice was born and raised in Pontiac, Michigan. She is a wife and mother.

Minister Brice currently holds a Masters and Bachelors of Science in Psychology and an Associate of Arts in Business from University of Phoenix.

Minister Brice received much of her ministerial foundation through servitude in her father's ministry (His Abiding Presence Ministries, Waterford, MI). In August 2009, Minister Brice received her ministerial license from Pastor, Dr. Marie E. Brice (Pentecostal Church of Deliverance, Baltimore, MD).

In 2007, Minister Brice began her evangelistic work preaching and assisting ministries and non-profit organizations in the Metro-Detroit, MI area. Minister Brice's desire is to aid individuals and families, especially women and children who are in crisis and to act in capacity as a Christian counselor, advocate, and mentor resulting in the development of Just-Blessed Enterprises [an affiliate of WofGod, Inc. a (501c3) organization under the direction of Overseer Trena D. Stephenson].

Services offered through Just-Blessed Enterprises include:
- *Counseling (marital, family-related, life-coaching, parental encouragement, & youth mentorship)*
- *Evangelistic Services: i.e. workshops, seminars, revivals and church related engagements.*
- *Organizational Leadership services.*
- *Outreach & Community Service*
- *Mentorship Training*

In addition to Minister Brice's educational accomplishments and ministerial endeavors, she is a writer and poet for JO Magazine. She is also a contributing author for "And He Still Sees" and "He Still Waits" compiled by Overseer Trena D. Stephenson (Daughters of Distinction, LLC & Women of God Ministries).

In retrospect, Minister Brice remains humbled by her accomplishments, yet maintains her first and more important work is to her family.

To contact Minister Brice direct all correspondence to: nattajblessed@gmail.com. Further information about Just-Blessed Enterprises is available at www.facebook.com/justblessed1 or by visiting wofgod.org.

Chapter 10

Unconditional Love

When speaking of unconditional love, usually discussion of the topic is from the angle of loving others unconditionally or God's unconditional love for us. However, I want to speak to you from a different angle. God gave me a life changing revelation birthed from my personal experience that has enhanced my relationship with God as well as how I serve in ministry. I believe that this great revelation from God will have as much of an impact on your life as it had on mine.

Earlier this year, I was obsessively zealous with working for the kingdom of God after discovering who I am in Christ. I sought to write, intercede, teach, and begin developing and walking in the spiritual gifts God endowed upon me. Everyday issues began to arise in my life and I found that I was not able to dedicate as much time to ministry and studying as much as I desired. My children needed extra attention at home, as they began to embrace their teenage years. My job was also in its busiest season and in a major transition. My obligations to the church as a leader required more time and accountability. Although my husband was very understanding and supportive, I knew I was slacking in my household responsibilities as other issues began to take priority.

Suddenly, my zeal and passion for pursuing what I believed

was the mission God set for my life, began to diminish because of being overwhelmed and burnt out. It became more of a burden than a life-fulfilling journey. My life began to seem meaningless and unproductive. I began questioning my abilities and even wondered if I just had too much on my plate at one time. As a result, I shut down my online Christian magazine (Heavenly Magazine) after questioning if in fact it was what God wanted me to do. Desperate for answers, I fell to my knees and begged God to show me the root of the problem. I asked Him to bring back the lost passion. Finding a balance and prioritizing seemed like an impossible fantasy at the time. After much fasting and prayer, I still had not heard an answer from the Lord.

    I continued living in a state of just existing and served in ministry out of habit and obligation but without power. It was the quietest yet most un-peaceful time in my life. I felt completely disconnected from God. Although my prayers, writing, and encouragement healed and set others free inside I was dying for my deliverance. I constantly cried out to God in desperation for change and was willing to do anything at that point! The desire to work in ministry and to live out my life's purpose was still a great desire in my heart. However, failure was an obvious sign that I missed something somewhere. I began to think that maybe I was going about it the wrong way.

    One day during prayer, the Lord showed me a vision of a branch lying on the ground with beautiful bright green leaves that slowly began to wither. It was lying next to a big and beautiful oak tree swaying gently with the wind. I heard the Holy Spirit say, you are the branch that fell to the ground. The longer you stay disconnected from me the faster you wither. I have never left you nor have I forsaken you (**Hebrews 13:5**). If you draw closer to me then I will draw closer to you (**James 4:8**). Tears began to stream down my face like a rushing river as I wept uncontrollably. I thought I was drawing closer to God. After all, I finally accepted my calling and was ready to carry out the ministry God gave me. However, look where that led me. My spiritual life was in a state of emergency and my natural life was not much better. On top of that, I did not have the slightest clue of how to draw closer to God after experiencing such an adverse effect to what I thought would keep me connected. God impressed II Chronicles 7:14 in my heart. ***"If my people, which are called by my name, shall humble themselves, and pray, and seek my face, and turn from their wicked ways; then will I hear from heaven, and will forgive their sin, and will heal their land."*** (KJV). I knew this was God's way of giving me clear and concise steps on how to draw closer to Him. He wanted me to reconnect with Him just as much as I wanted to be back in the loving relationship with Him I missed so much.

The vision of the little branch lying on the ground withering would not to leave my mind. It was like a movie constantly on replay. Repeating visions or dreams are a sign of urgency so I paid very close attention. In the vision, it was almost as if I was looking at myself from the view of a crane camera. In fact, I was looking at myself but from God's point of view. Although I gave up on Him, He never gave up on me. He waited patiently for me to reposition my mind, heart and spirit so that I could receive restoration to my rightful place in Him. His faithfulness, gentle kindness, and unconditional love lead me to humble myself, pray and repent. Afterward, I saw the leaves stop withering instantly. I saw what appeared to be rain falling from the oak tree as if it were crying. It drooped like a weeping willow as its tears of rain began to replenish the dry and partially withered leaves. I saw signs of life on the reviving yet still disconnected branch. The leaves began to slowly transition from brown and withered to orange ultimately turning vibrant green. His tears, the Lord's tears, were tears of joy and the signs of life were confirmation of His forgiveness of my sins and divine healing. Then, I saw what appeared to be a ray of light acting as gravity gently lifting the branch up and pulling it towards the oak tree. The newly rejoined branch began to rejoice with the rest of the leaves on the oak tree, rustling loudly in the wind like the sound of hands clapping and voices of praise exalting almighty God.

I lifted my hands and began to worship God with great appreciation, boldness, and confidence like never before. I was ever so grateful that He accepted me back into His body after having such ulterior motives. Again, I prayed but this time with a new perspective, and I was very honest with God about how I felt. "Lord, I still have a desire to work in your kingdom. The desire has not left, but this time I want to do things the way you want me to," I prayed. Almost immediately, He replied, "Why? Why do you want to work for my Kingdom?" He led me to James 4:3, *"When you ask, you do not receive, because you ask with wrong motives, that you may spend what you get on your pleasures."* (NIV). The reason my plan did not work out from the beginning is I had a motive problem. The motivation behind my desire to do greater works in the Kingdom of God was to have meaning in my life; to stop running from the mandate God had given me and to be used by God in a mighty and powerful way. The motivation should have been to glorify God.

The church of Ephesus worked hard, persevered, and was rich in good deeds. However, the Lord held one thing against them, they forgot about their first love (**Revelation 2:4**). They did not maintain the same zeal, love, and affection for God as they did when they first came into the knowledge of him. Jesus' warning to Ephesus was a call to repentance in that their minds, heart, and course of conduct would change. This was necessary so they could return to their first love or risk losing their brightness, which symbolized their connection to God and genuineness. God's warning to me was to repent for having the wrong motive. He told me to let unconditional love for Him become the motivation behind serving Him and His people. God knew exactly what to do to shut me down and place me in a season of brokenness so He could build me up on the proper foundation. The Kingdom work that needs finishing, in such a time as this, is far too great to risk because of selfishness. An end-time messenger's message must remain pure. After all, the foundation of the gospel message is love.

Jesus revealed to me that I could work in ministry, pray prayers that would cause healing for the sick and win all the souls in America. However, if I was not fulfilling the first and greatest commandment then for whom was I really working? My works would be in vain. A lawyer asked Jesus, "What is the greatest commandment in the law?" Jesus replied, *"Love the Lord your God with all your heart and with all your soul and with all your mind." The second is love your neighbor as yourself."* (Matthew 22:34-39 NIV). When a person loves God with all their heart, soul, and mind then serving His people, your fellow brothers, and sisters, out of genuine concern for their soul comes naturally and above your own motives. God told me to go back and accomplish the first commandment, to love God with all of my mind heart and soul.

I spent so many years of my spiritual life living in uncertainty while avoiding, denying, and being afraid of the calling God ordained for my life. There are people like me suffering through the greatest time of brokenness and just needing a word from God and encouragement. I allowed fear to set in and instead of turning away from fear to love; I turned from fear to work. I learned that fear is a sign of selfishness as well as a lack of faith and love. It shows that you are relying on your, not the Lord's knowledge and strength. It shows that you would rather protect yourself from embarrassment and exposure of lack of self-confidence than to step out in faith for the sake of bringing someone out of their current state and into a life-changing encounter with Jesus. God's must work through his people so that He is glorified here on earth but too many of us are being paralyzed with fear. *"There is no fear in love; but perfect love casteth out fear: because fear hath torment. He that feareth is not made perfect in love."* (I John 4:18 KJV).

Perfect love is to love God with all your soul, mind, and heart. How does one love God with all their soul, mind, and heart? God says love me as I love you. How do you do that? Love God unconditionally! There are two key factors in loving God unconditionally. First, unconditional love is faithful. Faithfulness does not permit cheating on God with sin. We are not perfect people but faithfulness will cause us to stay committed to the straight and narrow path God planned for our life. Faithfulness refuses to allow situations or people to cause us to waver in faith. Wavering faith is invoked by condition. We want to be full of faith not wavering in faith. The prerequisite to hearing the words "well done my good and faithful servant" is being faithful.

The second factor is unconditional love obeys. *"If ye love me, keep my commandments."* (John 14:15 KJV). If the Lord says speak, then speak. If the Lord says, do not do that; then do not do it. If God called you to intercede, intercede like your life depends on it. Stay true to your own convictions. Moses' disobedience cost him the blessing of seeing the "promised land." There are grave consequences to disobedience, which could cost you. It may prolong or forfeit your destiny or cause someone to miss the blessing God had for him or her through you. Moses' disobedience was a display that he did not trust God in that particular matter. Loving God is always having faith in Him; never giving up on Him and resting assuredly that loving God as He loves you will never fail! *"Nor height, nor depth, nor any other creature, shall be able to separate us from the love of God, which is in Christ Jesus our Lord"* (Romans 8:39 KJV) because we love Him unconditionally.

About The Author

Shinise Muse

Minister Shinise Muse is the wife to Deacon Gregory Muse and mother of three (Dayquale, Shayla and Patricia). She is a minister at Kingdom Harvest Ministries under the direction of Pastor Floyd E. Nelson II where she leads the Global Communications Department, is a Sunday school teacher and is a Tribal Leader with her husband. As a revivalist, worshiper and prophetic intercessor Minister Muse sits on the board of council members and is a part of the planning committee of the Prophetic Intercessors Council of an Empowered People (PICEP) founded by Elder Monique Simmons. She is the founder of the former Heavenly Magazine, an online spiritual growth Christian Magazine. As the Lord leads, she plans to one day begin again encouraging and teaching the saints through her passion for the written word and seeing the saints equipped and empowered to serve God and His people.

Chapter 11

Are You Truly Sold Out

God's grace imparted into my life has caused me to sell out completely to Jesus Christ. It was God's mercy, His forgiveness, compassion, longsuffering, tenderness, and His closeness that brought me from ashes, dust, hurts, pains, and love that had dried up like a dusty water brook. I wanted a man, my own husband, so desperately to love me.

One night (December 7, 1970) at 12 midnight a knock came at my door, it was Brother and Sister Arthur Conward, they heard that I wanted prayer. I was in desperate need of help. I tried to commit suicide by swallowing 26 pills all of different kinds, but the attempt was unsuccessful. My friends, Napoleon and Ruth Rhodes, saw my desperate need for help and sent these two wonderful, saved saints. Truly, God sent them to rescue my five girls and me. God and His divine providence were looking out for me.

I remember in September 1975, I took my youngest daughter Patrice to her first day of kindergarten and as I walked her to school, I was conversing to my God about my life. Things were not going the way I thought they should go. However, when I got home after taking her to school, the Holy Ghost gave me an experience that I will never forget. It seemed like the Lord baptized me all over again in the in Holy Ghost and with fire. With my face to the wall, tears flooding my face I told God these words, "Behold I am your handmaid, be it unto me according to thy word." The Lord spoke to me to be faithful until death.

Yes, I was facing a failed marriage. My husband finished medical school and I wanted so desperately to be that doctor's wife, but things started spiraling down. No begging or pleading could make him come to the realization that we could make our marriage work regardless of the intruders that he allowed to come in.

What caused me to be truly sold out to Jesus Christ? I developed a relationship with Jesus, by reading my bible daily, and seeking His face in prayer. I wanted to know Him just as He had apprehended and redeemed me. My sole desire was to know God with my whole heart.

God did not put me on earth to build a self- image of myself or to put anything or anyone before Him. God wanted my whole heart to love Him dearly. Can you imagine having children of your own and you bring in other children into your home and you give them more attention, more love, more gifts and then neglect your own children?! How do you think they will feel? Our God would feel the same way if we allow anyone or anything to take precedence over Him.

Many times, I have gone to the grocery store looking to buy a specific item and when I get to the aisle where the item should be on the shelf, guess what, the item is sold out. Therefore, you look around for an employee for assistance and ask, "when will this item be in stock again," and they tell you "we no longer carry that item." You are disappointed. So what do you do? You proceed to another store to find your item. My point is this, God is not happy when we, His children are not truly sold out to Him. Yes, it takes time to get in that place where Christ wants you to be, yet we must start with a true commitment to Him. If we start wrong, we will end up wrong.

Today, not too many saints are truly committed to God. They have a form of godliness but deny the power thereof according to scripture. In the old days, saints did not let anything hinder them from serving God. Truly selling out to Jesus means simply this: a <u>committed, dedicated life to Jesus Christ</u>. Most definitely, we are truly going to encounter many trials, tribulation, illness, or poverty.

Jesus makes this very clear in John 16:33, *"These things I have spoken unto you, that in me ye might have peace. In the world ye shall have tribulation: but be of good cheer; I have overcome the world."* (KJV).

Yes, we are told that Satan our enemy will do everything in his power to stop a child of God from following Jesus. The bible teaches us in John 10:29, *"My Father, which gave [them] me, is greater than all; and no man is able to pluck them out of my Father's hand."* (KJV). As believers, we are in the hands of Jesus. We have blessed assurance of God's word that He will protect us, and that He is greater than any force on the face of this earth. Furthermore, He will not allow anything or anyone to deceive or snatch us from him. Who wouldn't be SOLD OUT to a GREAT GOD that has given us His word to keep us from the destruction of Satan? The bible warns us that we are despised, rejected, and hated because we are followers of Jesus. Our strong determination is to go on and follow our Savior regardless of the cost.

Let me tell you about a healer named Jesus Christ. He is the great physician. His office is located in heaven and His central line is never busy. Psalm 107:20 (in part) says, *"And he sent his word and healed them."* (KJV). I personally know Jesus as a healer. I had my first open heart surgery October 2000, a five by-pass operation. Being very ill, I did not understand the danger I was in. Nevertheless, the Lord gave me an assuring word *"Ye shall not die but live to declare the works of the Lord,"* (Psalms 18:17 KJV). Nine months later, I was living in Miami, Florida pastoring a small church of believers. The Lord was truly with us. In January 2009, the illness returned and I again underwent, another surgery. I felt no fear because I knew my God was with me. The bible says, God will never leave us nor forsake us. What a promise! The Lord impressed upon me to return to Maryland to be with my family. In April 2009, the pain came back. Months later, in August 2009 I was admitted in the hospital. The doctors informed me that the physicians in Miami could not really fix the problem. They supposedly performed a two by-pass operation to fix the main artery, which were done incorrectly. The doctors at Adventist Hospital gave me less than a year to live if I did not have stents placed in my main artery. I agreed to the stents.

I suffered a great deal of pain while in the hospital. The

blood oozed unstoppably out of the wound. I spoke to the Lord and He answered me and said, "Jesus is on the main line tell him what you want." I made my request to God and immediately the blood stopped. Tell me God is not real! He sees, He hears and He will answer. I am a living witness. I was discharged out of the hospital and was given thirteen pills to take daily but my God, my loving God delivered me from thirteen pills to four pills daily. I am truly blessed. God said, "Be still and know I am God." I am a living testimony to many wonderful blessings God has bestowed upon me and for others to see that God can heal them too, only believe.

I look at my children, grandchildren, and great-grandchildren and I can truly say the blessings of God are upon us. Has it been easy for me during these forty years to be truly sold out to Jesus? Was it easy for me to say yes Lord all the time? I had my days of murmuring and complaining, but I learned through chastisement, rebukes, and correction to be submissive to a Holy God. Thanks to my God who loves me so much that He tells me in His word, **"Casting all your care upon him; for he careth for you."** (I Peter 5:7 KJV. That is the word and it works if we only trust him. A song writer named Charles Albert Tindley caught the vision and wrote a powerful song called "Nothing Between," It's powerful lyrics read

> *"Nothing between my Soul and the Savior, naught of this world's delusive dreams. I have renounced all sinful pleasures, Jesus is mine, and there's nothing between."*

Here is a short story I must tell you. Listen, problems will occur in the life of a child of God. There is no getting around it. They have calls on their lives and a destiny to fulfill. However, God will give them the grace to go through the obstacles and the perseverance to accomplish His will. It is said that John Bunyan wrote Pilgrims Progress from jail.

Florence Nightingale, too ill to move from her sick bed, re-organized the hospitals of England. Semi-paralyzed and under constant menace of apoplexy, Pasteur was tireless in his attacks on disease. Harriet Tubman refused to be a quitter. While she was only in her thirties, Harriet Tubman was called Moses because of her ability to go into the land of captivity and bring so many of her people out of slavery's bondages. She was truly sold out to the cause! The apostle known as John the Beloved was put on the Isle of Patmos because of his belief and testimony that Jesus is the Messiah. So many other apostles, disciples, Christians refused to denounce Jesus as their Lord and Savior. History tells us that the apostle Peter was crucified upside down because he was unworthy to be crucified right side up as Jesus. Nero's henchman beheaded Paul, the aged apostle, and Nero himself committed suicide in AD 68 because he saw the steadfastness of Paul and heard the testimonies of saints that were truly sold out to Jesus.

Bury a person in the snows of Valley Forge and you have a George Washington, raise him in abject poverty, and you have an Abraham Lincoln. Strike him down with infantile paralysis and he becomes a Franklin D. Roosevelt. Burn him so badly that the doctors say he will never walk again and you have a Glenn Cunningham, who set the world's one-mile record in 1934. If he or she is born black in a society filled with racial discrimination and you have a Booker T. Washington, a Marion Anderson, and a George Washington Carver, a Harriet Tubman or a Martin Luther King, Jr. Call him a slow-learner, retarded, and writing him off as uneducated, and you have an Albert Einstein. These all showed in their hard work that they were not lazy, slothful, nor jealous of each other's callings but were dedicated and committed to their callings. Yes, they all had their individual professions, duty, and struggles and yet remained faithful to their calling and anointing.

Finally, my desire is to please Jesus, my Lord and Savior for He alone transformed my life from darkness to his marvelous light. **"Let the word of Christ dwell in you richly in all wisdom"** (Colossians 3:16 KJV). If we allow the Holy Ghost to work in us, the righteousness of God will be witnessed in you and I. As a result, the world will know we are truly sold out to Jesus.

About The Author

Shirley Bryant

Overseer Shirley Bryant accepted Christ into her life December 7th, 1970. Not knowing the reality of serving Christ was real, she began reading the bible daily, and attending Saturday night prayer meeting services in the home of Brother Arthur and Sis. Mary Conward. In June 1971 at the prayer meeting services, she received the baptism of the Holy Ghost. Sis Bryant received much prayer, encouragement, and love from Bro. Arthur and Sis. Mary Conward while going through a divorce and raising 5 daughters. In 1973 while attending a Sunday Morning Service at People's Christian Church, she heard an audible voice of Jesus saying read St. Luke 4:18. It was then that Sis. Mary Conward told her that God had called and anointed her to preach the gospel. She served in different capacities in ministry as a Sunday School teacher, Church Secretary, and ordained Head Missionary under the auspices of Pastor Author Conward.

Overseer Bryant was ordained as an Evangelist in 1981. From that point on, with God being her strength, she was determined to do God's work. Evangelist Bryant was a faithful member at Peoples Christian Church in Washington, D.C. In August 2001, she moved to her hometown, Miami, Florida, evangelizing young people and their parents. It was joy unspeakable and full of glory to see them come in her backyard to hear the gospel of Jesus. In May 2006, Evangelist Bryant was ordained a Pastor and Living by Faith Deliverance Ministry birthed in Miami, Florida and many came to hear the gospel preached. In April 2008, she received a certificate in Biblical Studies from Thomas Brown Bible College. Pastor Shirley A. Bryant is currently serving as an Overseer at Faith International Church. Truly, God is in her life.

Overseer Bryant is completely sold out to Jesus Christ and there's no turning back. There is more work for her to do and the love of God compels her to go forward in whatever he assigns to her hands to do. Her Motto is "Experiencing the Difference Christ Will Make in Your Life"

Chapter 12

And He Still Waits

As I ponder in thought, I asked God what He would have me to say to our readers. As we culminate this series, the only biblical story that came to mind was the parable of the lost son found in Luke 15. It reads,

<u>The Parable of the Lost Son</u>
[11] Jesus continued: "There was a man who had two sons. [12] The younger one said to his father, 'Father, give me my share of the estate.' So he divided his property between them. [13] "Not long after that, the younger son got together all he had, set off for a distant country and there squandered his wealth in wild living. [14] After he had spent everything, there was a severe famine in that whole country, and he began to be in need. [15] So he went and hired himself out to a citizen of that country, who sent him to his fields to feed pigs. [16] He longed to fill his stomach with the pods that the pigs were eating, but no one gave him anything. [17] "When he came to his senses, he said, 'How many of my father's hired servants have food to spare, and here I am starving to death! [18] I will set out and go back to my father and say to him: Father, I have sinned against heaven and against you. [19] I am no longer worthy to be called your son; make me like one

of your hired servants.' [20] *So he got up and went to his father. "But while he was still a long way off, his father saw him and was filled with compassion for him; he ran to his son, threw his arms around him and kissed him.* [21] *"The son said to him, 'Father, I have sinned against heaven and against you. I am no longer worthy to be called your son.'* [22] *"But the father said to his servants, 'Quick! Bring the best robe and put it on him. Put a ring on his finger and sandals on his feet.* [23] *Bring the fattened calf and kill it. Let's have a feast and celebrate.* [24] *For this son of mine was dead and is alive again; he was lost and is found. So they began to celebrate. (Luke 15:11-24 NIV)*

Often the above passage of scripture is taught and used to make an appeal to a believer who is in a backslidden state or condition. Backslidden refers to one who knows God and obtains a relationship with God but chooses to walk away from God for personal reasons such as lust of the flesh, greed or just merely not wanting to submit to Gods plans for our lives. However, what appears overlooked are the disappointments we can experience in life. Subsequently, in anger of the life struggles we turn away from God.
Let me share just one of my life struggles. I was raised up in the church and my parents instilled great values in me such as being independent and successful. They taught me not to depend on a man for happiness but to find happiness with myself. These are just a few of the things they instilled in me. I had a very outgoing personality. I was very active as a believer, and I loved going out and sharing the gospel to the less fortunate. I especially enjoyed working with my father at the Red Cross and feeding the homeless. In the midst of all the excitement of life when I reached my senior year in high school, I moved from Texas to live in Germany. I grew up in a military family. So we moved often.

After arriving in Germany, I met someone and fell head over heels in love. He would take me on long romantic walks in the park, buy me roses, essentially wine and dine me. This was the man of my dreams I felt so loved, safe and secure. My family loved and accepted him. After all, my sister introduced us. I thought he was perfect for me. I thought I did all the right things. I met his family and was around them often. I observed how he treated his mom, whom he treated very well. I was often told that seeing the way a man treats his mom is true indication of how he will treat his wife.

We dated for about a year and half before we married. I remember the day I left from home I was full of excitement of what life would be with him. I was so mystified and in love, I had no idea what was about to happen, once I reached his location. I left my father's house a place of refuge, abundance and peace. This was a place I did not have a care in the world. I chose to leave and chase a dream that would never become my realty. Can you imagine flying all the way from Germany leaving your family which is all you know for the majority of your life to start a new life with someone else? It was scary but I was ready. I thought life was going to be nothing but a bed of roses not realizing that thorns are located on the stem of the rose. I learned quickly that life has high and low moments. Although I missed my family greatly, I was excited about my new life to come.

Unfortunately, what I thought would be forever was not. I was married to someone who was emotionally abusive and eventually became physically abusive. My carefree spirit was crushed because of statements made to me by the one I loved. Going in public was scarce; there were rarely times I went out of the house. I looked to the floor when another man passed by me because if I looked in his direction I was scolded. I went from carefree to caged. I went from independent to being dependent. I was confined and isolated. There was no bus system to go places. My only mode of transportation was if he took me. My world began falling apart very fast. Here I was saved, filled with the Holy Ghost, loved God, but as soon as my world began to crash, I blamed God.

In the midst of the turmoil, I found out, I was pregnant. I was happy with the idea of being a mom but I did not like the circumstances. I was so unhappy. I recall one day when my parents came from Germany for a visit. My daughter had just been borne and I was so happy they were there. One night as we prepared to go to bed, we got in an argument, which was usual, but this night it was different. He was so angry with me. I remember asking him to pass me the pillow as we lay down. Instead, he did not pass it. He placed it over my face and pressed down to smother me. Then he finally released his hold. At that point, I was in shock. OMG, what had I truly gotten myself into. After that incident, I said to myself enough is enough. I packed a small bag of items for me and my daughter and moved out.

At that point, I found myself in the lowest place in my life. I thought to myself God what am I going to do now. I just had a baby. My daughter was not even six months old. I had no source of income. I was not working at all, but I found a place for us to live – boy, what a shock! I never expected I would have to live in a place like that let alone with my newborn baby. At least we had somewhere to go. After I moved, I decided to return to my old apartment a week later to retrieve the remainder of our things, but that did not happen. I arrived to the apartment to unlock the door my key did not work. I went to the rental office to find out he changed the locks on the doors. All I had was what I originally left with the week before.

I would cry out to God, "why is this happening to me?" "I'm a good person, why God why?" In my frustration, I began to shut down on life. I went to church but what I once found fun was no longer fun but a chore to me. I stayed depressed and I was angry with God. I merely existed. I still prayed and paid my tithes and served in the church. However, I was numb and had given up on life. I soon realized God was looking at my heart not my actions. After my pity party was over, I decided I needed God so much more than I needed Him before. I asked God to forgive me for being angry and distancing myself from His presence. I begin to chase God vigorously. I began to rebuild my prayer life and my worship unto Him. I fell in love with God all over again. Then one night as I was in prayer, the fog lifted. I came to the realization I left home too soon.

I needed to learn and experience more. I was not as grown as I thought although I was married at the tender age of 19. Boy, talk about a WOW moment. For many days, I pondered if my parents would allow me to return home. Finally, I worked up the nerve to call my dad. When I heard my dad's voice I began to weep "Daddy, daddy can I come back home?" Without hesitation my dad said "When we return stateside I will allow you to move back home." Well six months passed and my dad's assignment in Germany was finally over. My parents arrived back stateside and moved to Maryland. Just as my dad promised, I received the call from him saying I'm coming to get you and bring you back home. My dad traveled 10 hours by car to come get me. My daughter and I loaded up in the car to head home. I was so happy and relieved.

When I got home, I was so broken I did not even know who Trena was anymore. I lost myself somewhere along the way. One day my parents heard me crying in my room and they came in the room to speak to me. My dad said "Your mom and I are behind you 100%. You will be ok. I began to discover who I was again. I was not how I use to be, but so much better. I became stronger, secure and at peace with life and myself. Most of all, my love for God continued to grow leaps and bounds. I knew without any doubt I made the right decision for my daughter and me. That is my story. What is yours?

You can walk close to God and perform many works for Him. Yet your heart is far from Him. Many people who would pass by us daily would not even know that we backslid from God. Why, because we continue in church as usual. When God spoke that message to me, I was dumbfounded. I said "Lord I continued to worship you and spent time in prayer. What do you mean I was in a backslidden state?" The Lord clearly said "Trena what was your tone in prayer to me during that time. You cried out to me in anger blaming me for your misfortunes. I promised to never leave you nor forsake you. However, you left me." The Lord began to reveal that I limited my time with Him. I remember many nights praying unto the Lord for hours on end sometimes to the point I would fall asleep in His presence. I totally lost complete track of time and boy let us not talk about times of worship. My worship time with God was so intense not just in church but home as well. I would sit on the couch hours on end listening to one worship song after the other. Loving on God and telling Him how much He meant to me. I was so grateful.

What once motivated me to serve God had dwindled away. Think about it. Do you pray as you use too? Do you worship as you use too? Are you still the first one to arrive to church and the last one to go home? On the other hand, are you arriving late and leaving early? Do you run to or away from the altar for prayer? Do you know you are hurting but not wanting anyone one to know you are hurting? Have you reached out for counsel or have you chosen to avoid counsel that could be of help to you? Are you in a place where you find yourself just existing not surviving? To exist is just functioning without drive, meaning you stick to your routine not wanting to create change but stay the same. When we turn from God because of disappointment, we lose our drive to survive. Boy there were many times in my life when I can recall existing and not surviving, how about you. Where are you in life's equation? Do you exist in life internally or just externally? You know how we do sometimes. We can check out at any time. I can be in a room and many people are talking all around me and sometimes directly to me, but I tune out the voices and act as if I am the only one in the room. How many times have you checked out on God emotionally or spiritually because of a disappointment or wound? The Lord says: **"These people come near to me with their mouth and honor me with their lips, but their hearts are far from me. Their worship of me is made up only of rules taught by men."** (Isaiah 29:13 NIV).

Wow what a powerful scripture. Please be real and honest with yourself. Are you in a backslidden condition because of life struggles? If you find yourself in any part of my story, God is waiting for you to return to Him. He will not judge you but receive you with open arms and love. God is waiting with your robe in hand, and blessings that will overtake you. Those blessings are far greater than what you had before, much greater, a more intense bond, full of prayer and continual worship!

Pray this prayer with me.
Daddy God, Please forgive me for from walking away from you emotionally and spiritually. I repent now! I ask that you fully restore me emotionally and, spiritually. I receive now your love, favor and blessings much greater than before. I thank you for never leaving me alone. You consistently stayed by my side always. Thank you for hearing and receiving my prayer, that I send up in much humility and love. It is in Jesus name I pray Amen!

Now God says to you, "My child I have been waiting all this time. Welcome home, welcome home!

About The Author

Overseer Trena Stephenson

Overseer Trena Stephenson is a glorious, compassionate, humble and loving woman of GOD. She exemplifies the Lord in faith and good works. Her constant walk with the Lord allows her to minister to the heart, heal the wounded and reconcile the lost back to God. Born and raised in the church, the Lord entered and influenced her life early under the ministry of her parents, Pastor (Chaplain) Charles Jackson and First Lady Nina Jackson. Trena answered the call of ministry in 1993. She is a gifted preacher, teacher, worship leader, author, playwright and intercessor.

Overseer Trena Stephenson was ordained as a prophetess at Radical Apostolic Power International Ministries under the leadership of Senior Pastor Antonio Briggs. She was ordained as Elder through Bibleway Churches of America Worldwide under the Presiding Prelate and Chief Apostle Cornelius Showell. In December 2010, Overseer Stephenson was elevated to the office of overseer of Woman of God, Inc. The mission of Woman of God Ministries is to bring women into the fullness of what God has for them and their ministries. Overseer Stephenson is a mentor to a diverse group of women whose walk in the Lord is as different as the denominational ministries they serve.

Daughters of Distinction, was birthed in 2008, based off her passion for writing and helping others. She is a visionary, a woman of great faith, compassion, and integrity. She has been the guest speaker on "The Wenda Royster Show," a radio broadcast of Radio One; Rejoice TV Network; TBN, and Preach the Word Network. In April 2008, Overseer Stephenson became the Executive Producer and Creative Director for Daughters of Distinction TV, which houses two shows Daughters of Distinction Live and Let's Talk a new show that launched in April 2011. Both shows air on Rejoice TV Network in MD and DC. On May

7, 2011, Overseer Stephenson launched The Fullness of God Radio Broadcast airing in AL, PA, FL, LA, and GA. In September 2010, Overseer Trena launched Soar Magazine and online magazine to empower and encourage the people of God.

When God opens the door for Overseer Stephenson, she walks through it under the Anointing of the Holy Spirit with the purpose of leading someone to Christ. She has ministered throughout the United States as well as overseas in locations such as Poland, Paris, and various cities in Germany. Her ability to relate and touch God's children in all walks of life is truly a blessing.

Overseer Stephenson is also a wonderful mother to her daughter, Trea Stephenson. She has many spiritual children who love and respect her. Her Love for the Lord is truly a blessing and is demonstrated by the lives she touches in her church home and community.
www.wofgod.org
www.dofdllc.com
www.soarmagazine.info

When One Journey Ends, Another One Begins....

Well dear readers this is the last book to the book series entitled The Fullness of God. I pray that through each book you have been encouraged and enlighten on what the fullness of God really means.

We started with letting you know that "He Still Hears." No matter what you are going through, do not ever think God does not hear you because He does. Then we moved on to find out "He Still Speaks"… but the true question is if we are listening attentively? Rather, is our own voice drowning out the voice of God? Then we came along with the third book to the series "And He Still Sees." There is nothing new under the sun. When you do not think God sees, He does. He sees what we do in public but most of all, what we do behind closed doors. When God looks upon us is He pleased or disturbed. This final book, "And He Still Waits" speaks on our God waiting for us to come to Him. This is a book of reconciliation between man and God. We all have fallen short in some area of our life. However, I thank God that no matter what, He is waiting to receive me unto Himself. People of God do not give up and do not give in. Study the word of God. The word of God speaks to all areas of our life no matter what it is. Remember when you approach God He will love you, rebuke you, encourage you, and heal you and whatever the need is He will meet it. As I stated this journey ends but another begins.

In 2012, we are launching a seven part book series entitled "Seven Ingredients of An Effective Prayer Life. " This series will teach you the different dimensions and postures in prayer. I pray you will continue to follow Daughters of Distinction, LLC as we continue to explore the different facets of God. We will continue to grow together, cry together and laugh together.

I love you more than you will even know!
Trena

Releases from Daughters of Distinction

Introducing the Series Entitled "The Fullness of God"

I.   And He Still Hears   II.   And He Still Speaks

III.   And He Still Sees   IV.   And He Still Waits

To learn more about the services and upcoming releases go to www.dofdllc.com

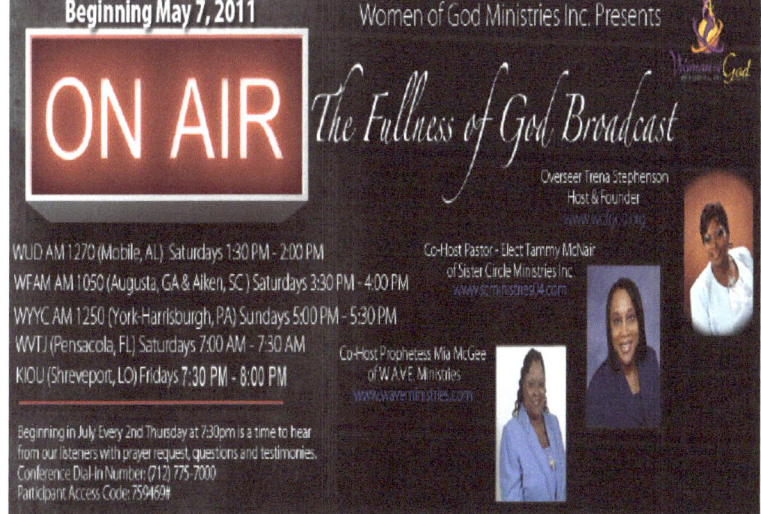

References

"Disciple." Dictionary.com Unabridged. Random House, Inc. 28 June. 2011. <Dictionary.com http://dictionary.reference.com/browse/disciple>.

"Disciple." Easton's 1897 Bible Dictionary. 28 June. 2011. <Dictionary.com http://dictionary.reference.com/browse/disciple>.

"Fan." Dictionary.com Unabridged. Random House, Inc. 29 Sep. 2011. <Dictionary.com http://dictionary.reference.com/browse/fan>.

Williams, Andy. "Nothing Between." Born Free/Love Andy. Sony/ATV Publishing, 1966.

Clifford Larson, Kate. Bound For the Promised Land. New York: One World Books, 2004.

"Image." Bing.com. Encarta World English Dictionary [North American Edition]. 29 Sep. 2011. <http://www.bing.com/Dictionary/search?q=define+image&qpvt=definition+image+&FORM=DTPDIA>.

"Dominion." Bing.com. Encarta World English Dictionary [North American Edition]. 29 Sep. 2011. <http://www.bing.com/Dictionary/search?q=define+dominion&go=&form=QB>.

"Bless." Bing.com. Encarta World English Dictionary [North American Edition]. 29 Sep. 2011. <http://www.bing.com/Dictionary/search?q=define+bless&form=QB>.

"Await." Farlex, Inc., 2011. Retrieved July 19, 2011 from http://www.thefreedictionary.com/awaiting.

Tindley, Charles Albert. "Nothing Between." Charles Albert Tindley, 1906.